Redfish

Redfish

All You Need to Know About Where, When & How to Catch Reds

Pete Cooper, Jr.

The Countryman Press
Woodstock, Vermont

With time, access points, signs, and landmarks referred to in
this book may be altered. If you find that such changes have
occurred in the places described in this book, please let the author
and the publisher know so that corrections may be made in
future editions. The author and publisher also welcome other
comments and suggestions. Address all correspondence to:

Editor
The Countryman Press
P.O. Box 748
Woodstock, VT 05091

© 2008 by Pete Cooper, Jr.

ISBN 978-0-88150-788-1

Cover design by Johnson Design, Inc.
Book design and composition by Faith Hague
Interior photographs by the author
Front cover photograph by Capt. Bubby Rodriguez

Published by The Countryman Press,
P.O. Box 748, Woodstock, Vermont 05091

Distributed by W. W. Norton & Company, Inc.,
500 Fifth Avenue, New York, NY 10110

Printed in the United States of America

10 9 8 7 6 5 4 3 2 1

To Barbara,
life-mate, soulmate,
and a pretty damn good
redfisherman, too!

Contents

Prologue

Over the years, folks' perspectives on red drum—ol' *Sciaenops ocellatus*—have changed radically. In places where these fish share the water with creatures that are slightly more pleasing to the palate, they were once second-rate targets that received the directed efforts of comparatively few anglers. Conversely, in areas where proper skillet material isn't normally as plentiful, reds have been a major topic of interest for generations. However, these days it seems that throughout their entire range they rate right up there with the best of 'em.

Undoubtedly that's at least in part because more folks have learned how to cook 'em decently.

Whatever the case, reds also provide a very accessible source of fine fishing entertainment from south Texas to the Chesapeake Bay and in water ranging in salinity from 0 ppt (that's fresh water, folks!) to seawater at approximately 35 ppt, and even much higher than that in the hypersaline Laguna Madre. And that can occur almost—if not entirely—year-round. Redfish are truly great fun to catch—strong, dogged fighters that will occasionally make a very spirited sprint—and, usually, they don't require degrees in quantum physics or fisheries biology to catch.

While writers of recreational fishing lore tend to use non-committal words like "usually," "normally," "often," and "sometimes" to protect their butts in case a pattern they have described doesn't work, I avow the last statement is true to the letter. That is because I was educated in neither physics nor biology but have caught more than 10,000 of the copper-plated beasts. Incidentally, almost a thousand of them—along with my largest one—fell to flies!

That statement is intended to add something to my credibility in creating these lines. It was assuredly in no way whatsoever ever intended to be a boast, me being a relatively humble sort of guy. I'm pretty sure that just about anyone else could compile a similar tally—if they could fish for them four days a week year-round for 40-odd years. If, perchance, extenuating circumstances (like a real job) might prevent them from doing so, they can use the data herein to very good purpose.

They might enjoy reading about it all, too.

First Redfish

Throughout my early life, I spent one or two weeks every summer on extended fishing trips in Rockport, Texas—a time-honored getaway for my parents and grandparents back then, but I was 20 before I caught my first redfish. Specks were our singular target, and we fished for them religiously from my maternal grandfather's 16-foot Magnolia, mostly while drifting across the beds of turtlegrass in Aransas Bay outside of Traylor Island. It was fun, and each trip was eagerly anticipated—though almost as much for the resulting fast-fried fillets as for the sport of acquiring them. However, by my late teens the tales told by the locals, the pictures on the marinas' walls, and the dead fish in the ice bins of the fish houses had honed my desire to catch reds to a very sharp edge.

In 1964, my grandfather and I stayed at Rockport for several days after my parents and sisters had returned to our home in Shreveport. We had taken a few fair specks before they left, but things had been a little slow in our regular proven spots along the island. And we were hearing some very good reports from Cedar Bayou, a deep cut separating San José Island from Matagorda Island and at the time linked Mesquite Bay to the Gulf.

That was a long way from where we normally fished, but Granddaddy was game to give it a try. We launched the boat that unforgettable morning at a very shallow ramp near the mouth of Copano Bay and headed that way up the Intercoastal Canal with great expectations—and no small amount of wonder at the big sign we soon came across on the side of the canal proclaiming HARVEY, LA. – 612 MILES! With the aid of a crudely drawn map—and with a lot of good luck—we missed the shallow reefs in the bay and eventually found ourselves in a cut of beautifully green water surrounded by the most promising turtlegrass flats I had ever seen. Gulls were in a frenzy, squawking and diving on shrimp being herded to the water's surface by a strike-a-cast school of specks. Granddaddy was ecstatic, but after we had boxed 20 or so of them, I could no longer resist the allure of those gorgeous flats. Armed with a box full of spoons and a couple of topwater bass plugs, I abandoned the specks, went overboard, and began my first serious quest for reds.

The flats were about a foot deep, with a relatively hard bottom, and with scattered small and large patches of grass. In the distance, the vegetation created dark splotches in the crystalline water, and on closer inspection its edges teemed with a marvelous abundance of marine life: shrimp, minnows, crabs, an occasional spooked flounder, and—redfish? I could not believe what I was looking at! A mere hundred yards from Granddaddy's boat, I was staring at a red that was no more than 20 feet from me, rooting through the grass. Then all my youthful talent for pinpoint casting learned in the often extremely tight confines of the cypress brakes that dotted the lakes near home vanished in an instant as my cast backlashed and dropped the surface lure I was speculating right on top of the fish, which immediately spooked. I almost cried!

An hour or so later, having covered about a quarter of a square mile of very promising water, I hadn't seen another fish. But as I made my way back to the boat, I encountered a fine flounder swimming easily across an open patch of sandy bottom. This time the cast with the surface lure was on the mark, the fish struck, I struck back—and missed it! I was sick—it was the biggest flounder I had ever seen!

Thoroughly rattled now, I wasn't paying attention to what was around me as I turned to continue on to the boat and almost collided with a school of three redfish. Unbelievably, they didn't spook, and at a distance of no more than 15 feet I made a sidearm lob at the biggest one. It immediately struck, and for an instant I thrilled to the previously unknown power in a red's initial run. Then the hooks pulled, and for a very long time I stood there motionless, alone on a Texas turtlegrass flat, wrapped in despair unlike any other I had ever felt while fishing.

Back at the boat, I found that Granddaddy had taken about 15 more rather smallish specks. As we chatted about the recent activities on our way back to the launch site, I could sense he was not in favor of returning, even after hearing my rather overwhelming story of the reds at least twice. Back in Rockport, having eaten a light lunch at Kline's and settled in for our daily afternoon nap, our discussion of the morning's happenings became a little more heated, and I regret what I said and how I said it to this day. True, I had been eye-to-eye with the first redfish I had ever seen alive, and a passion to catch one had been burning inside me for several years. But because of that I became disrespectful—even impudent—to the man who had influenced me the most in becoming a fisherman. I think I realized and regretted that at the time, but there was something within me that I just couldn't hold back, and for the only time I can ever remember, we went to sleep mad at each other.

After the nap—and with a very unfamiliar and very uncomfortable air between us—I headed out for my normally unproductive afternoon wade-fishing session along the old town's waterfront. There, while working the sparse grass patches and the washouts around the piers' pilings with a spoon, I had one strike—a sudden surge, a screech from the reel's drag, and then a broken line.

That evening at dinner, subtly making me feel like the most ungrateful child that I was, but not saying it in so many words, Granddaddy mentioned that he felt he could have caught more fish that day if he had been a little quicker on the strike and wondered if I wanted to go back to Cedar Bayou again in the morning. And for that effort, my beloved grandfather left one more footprint on the edges of the bays in my life.

I did not sleep well that night. Guilt and excitement do not make for restful slumber, and I was awake long before the alarm went off. We had the boat in the water at daybreak, and 45 minutes later we were anchored off the head of the bayou in a clear, rising tide and with fish everywhere. I did not even try for the specks that morning, and as soon as the boat was secured, I wished Granddaddy good luck and headed off on my quest.

The tide was higher, the sun a little lower, and the bottom seemingly a little softer that morning as I made my way across the grass. Another fisherman, working a popping rig with a live shrimp, had caught one, but I did not see a fish for two hours. Then, once again on my way back to the boat, one waved its tail at me from the middle of a large patch of grass. The cast to it with the surface lure was good, the fish struck, and a short time later I had my redfish—almost 4½ pounds. And I didn't think I could be happier until it brought a smile from Granddaddy.

Although he and I were to fish together at Rockport for several more years, that was the last trip we made to Cedar Bayou— hallowed grounds that I've been told no longer exist. The lure—a perch-colored wooden Devil's Horse—was glued to a small plaque that for over 40 years graced a wall of an apartment and then of the loft of our house beneath John P. Cowan's first Gulf Coast Conservation Association (GCCA) print of a wade fisherman casting into a school of reds on a Texas turtlegrass flat. The red—thanks in great part to a grandfather's love for a 20-

After a lifetime and thousands of reds, they still bring a big smile to the author.

year-old child—signaled the beginning of a love for the species that remains to this day, even after having caught such numbers of them, many—as might be imagined—on surface lures. And the lure, I am exceedingly happy to relate, as well as the print, were rescued unharmed from the devastation that Hurricane Katrina wreaked upon our home.

As an aside, two years later I carried a fly rod to the Texas coast for the first time since 1958—the year I caught my first, and at the time my only, saltwater fish on a fly. On a solo trip late one uncharacteristically calm morning while wading the turtlegrass flats on the outside of Traylor Island, I caught my first red on a fly. It wasn't big—perhaps 20 inches long, and I do not recall what fly did it in, though I suspect it was some weathered facsimile of a streamer. It was not, I am almost certain, a popper—the type of fly that led to most of the reds I have taken since then.

That old Devil's Horse was a really good teacher, wasn't it?

Inshore

CHAPTER 1

The Marsh

The biological profile of red drum can be gotten from Google as well as the fish and game departments of all states that include waters where these fish are found. Very generally, redfish begin life during summer and early fall in the surf near the mouths of large coastal bays and sounds. Strong rising tides soon carry them into these estuarine nurseries, where they will pass roughly four years—virtually bulletproof to certain external stimuli, I might add. Around then—give or take a year or so—they will make a piecemeal migration to offshore waters, where they will join the breeding stock. There they can live to a ripe old age, make plenty of babies that will basically follow the same pattern of development, and if you need any more scientific scoop than that, look somewhere else. That is more than enough background for a sound beginning here!

The waters within interior salt and brackish marshes across virtually the entire Gulf Coast and a good part of the Atlantic hold red drum throughout most, if not all, of the year. With a few exceptions, these are juvenile fish, and I promise that at times they can appear to be slightly less intelligent than a similar-sized clod of dirt. However, that doesn't mean that they are consistently pushovers—far from it. Their developmental conditioning is entirely the result of this environment—its hazards and its havens—and the main reason why so many anglers can have a bit of trouble successfully fishing here. So if you are one of these anglers but would like to solve the riddle and experience the exciting action found in these areas, try the following tips.

Follow The Tide

Interior marshes are typically comprised of broad stands of various emergent grasses pocked with shallow ponds—with or without submergent grasses—and laced with small, shallow creeks and cuts. As the tide rises, it floods areas such as shallow, grass-choked ponds and shoreline vegetation along the cuts and creeks—feeding grounds that have been inaccessible to various prey species during the recent low-water period. Those creatures now move into these nutrient-rich areas, and the redfish follow.

In interior areas, it is almost always best to follow the fish into the shallowest water where you can operate your boat. As the tide continues to rise, look for shallower spots. Water more than $1\frac{1}{2}$ feet deep quickly becomes a detriment, as it masks many indications of a redfish's presence, and general blind-casting in these waters is typically much less effective than casting at indications of fish.

Periods of slack tide—either on the low end or the high end—are usually best spent taking a nap or returning to the marina for a snack. Just be sure you are back in operation when the water begins to move again. When it starts to fall, target the creeks and cuts.

These can be worked effectively by either using a trolling motor to move slowly along their shorelines where the falling water is pulling prey from the recently flooded grass, or by anchoring at the point where a cut drains a pond. There, the current created by the water falling through the cut pulls prey from the pond. Redfish are well conditioned to these feeding stations.

One note of caution, though. During times of extreme tidal ranges—or during the low end of the falling stage—do not let yourself get caught in a position where your boat can become grounded. Assuredly that can be a risk, especially when you are on fish and are focusing on more immediate activities. Just remember that even a 16-foot Kevlar Florida flats boat doesn't push-pole very well across liquid mud—and not at all across damp sand. I know!

Use The Stealth Mode

As a rule, redfish aren't all that bright, and some of them can act like they are eaten up with a really bad case of the dumb-ass. However, if you assume that those fish you encounter in the marshes are so afflicted, you won't catch many of them.

You must move about very stealthily while fishing shallow ponds and creeks. Paddling is best, if your boat allows it. Push-poling ranks a close second and provides better visibility, but it's rather difficult to make a quick, accurate cast with a 16-foot push-pole in one hand. Unless there's a buddy aboard who is willing to alternate rod and push-pole with you, paddle—sculling while sitting on the boat's bow—if at all possible.

If you are averse to paddling, if the water's depth is sufficient, and if there isn't a profusion of submergent grass in the area, a bow-mounted trolling motor can be used effectively *if* it is set on the lowest speed that will produce headway and *if* you thereafter *leave it alone!* Got that?

Whatever method of propulsion you decide on, go slowly. While that will allow you to search for fish more effectively, the main reason is to prevent the boat from creating large pulses through the water that can be detected by the fish, alerting them that something ain't quite right. Reds will often simply swim out of the way of a boat that is just creeping along, not in the least bit alarmed. Others that are caught unaware may bolt, but after they dash off a ways they occasionally seem to forget what all the fuss was about. A cast at fish that respond to the boat's presence in either of these ways can result in strikes you would not have received had your boat been pushing water and alerting them.

Look For Fish

One of the most exciting things about fishing the waters within interior marshes is that much of it is done by sight. As you move along (stealthily), you should always be looking and listening for signs of fish.

A large wake moving slowly along the bank of a small, off-clear pond or creek could be caused by one of several types of non-redfish found in these waters, but it is definitely worth a speculative cast. A much better bet is the tip of a tail intermittently puncturing the water's surface beside a patch of submergent grass. An entire tail waving merrily at you anywhere you might encounter one is almost a sure thing.

Then there are "crawlers"—fish that move with some purpose in water so thin that their dorsal fins and part of their backs are exposed. These fish might also appear to be almost a sure thing, but they demand a very precise cast. Unlike a "tailer," which is a stationary target, a crawler must be led just far enough to prevent the lure's impact from spooking the fish, yet close enough for the fish to detect it. Knowing just how much to lead it is determined in great part by experience, the phase of the moon, and blind dumb luck! Do not expect consistent results with crawlers—but then, that's what makes fishing for them such a hoot.

Your wardrobe can play an important role in your efforts at sight-fishing. Two of the most important factors are polarized

sunglasses with either amber or yellow lenses and a cap with a long bill that is either black or dark green on its underside. In clear water, you can detect redfish relatively easily beneath the surface. For best results, work the upwind shorelines where emergent vegetation creates a calm surface. Move along in the direction allowing the best subsurface visibility. If you are moving along slowly and stealthily, these fish can suddenly appear quite near the boat, so be prepared for a short, quick cast with minimal movement. Learn to flip-cast side-arm with reasonable accuracy if you can't already, since a rod waving—and reflecting sunlight—well above the water's surface is lifetime guaranteed to send them scurrying.

Barbara, to whom this book is dedicated. She caught the fish, too!

Prospect Irregularities

On first inspection, a pond, creek, or cut may seem to be relatively featureless. This is frequently not the case. Irregularities normally abound and are often quite attractive to prey species seeking nourishment or shelter, and redfish are likely to be nearby.

Small grass points in a creek's shoreline may extend into water which is slightly deeper than that found along the adjacent bank. Here any current may be slightly stronger, causing prey being carried along by it some disadvantage. These features make good ambush points and should be prospected with a cast or two wherever they are found. They do depend, though, on moving water – either way.

So do intersections, especially when one cut is much different from the other – smaller, shallower, more meandering, and so forth. These are usually best on a falling tide, but they can be productive during the low end of a rising tide. Target the shoreline shallows a short distance from the intersection itself.

During low tide, you may notice some shells on the bank of a creek. These may extend well out into the waterway, providing protection for prey species, especially at this time. Never pass up an accumulation of shoreline shells without making a cast or two across the water next to them. More on this in a later chapter.

Finally, reds may be found anywhere in ponds where the bottom is carpeted with thinly growing submergent grasses, but places where the grass grows in thick patches—often matting on the surface—tend to localize the fish. Take plenty of time scrutinizing—and prospecting—a pond with clumps of matted grass scattered throughout it.

Use Small, "Loud" Lures

One of the hottest lures going these days for reds in interior marshes is the Spoon Fly. It isn't really a fly, but it was created for fly-fishing folks, and it does look and act almost exactly like a miniature Johnson Sprite spoon! It is very light so it sinks quite slowly, it is created with a mono weed guard, it wobbles and flashes about, emitting audible as well as visible indications of a baitfish, and it is just about $1\frac{1}{4}$ inches long. Yeah, that's pretty small, but the redfish absolutely love it!

The above is not necessarily intended to coerce you into fly fishing for reds, but to encourage you to use the lures that are most appropriate for them in this setting—fairly small and "loud." In clear water, a $\frac{1}{5}$-ounce, single-hook spoon can be a good choice. Over the years, silver, feathered Tony Accetta Pet Spoons, Size 13, have accounted for a pile of my reds. In areas where submergent grass poses a problem, try a small buzzbait. In the slightly deeper (but not too deep!) cuts and creeks where submergent grass is not a factor, junior-sized surface lures can produce some very entertaining strikes. But day in and day out, if I absolutely had to catch redfish in the marsh, I would rely on a spinnerbait created from a gold, Size $3\frac{1}{2}$ Hildebrandt safety-pin spinner, a $\frac{1}{8}$-ounce jig-head with a stout, short-shanked size 2/0 hook, and a $2\frac{1}{2}$-inch grub—probably clear chartreuse with glitter. With that, I can make a relatively delicate presentation to a crawler, "buzz" it past a tailer at the edge of a thick patch of grass, and prospect the intersections, points, and accumulations of shells along a creek's shoreline.

I've been doing all that with quite satisfactory success for more than 35 years now, and see no reason whatsoever to change anything. Try these tips—you'll find that reds in the marsh aren't nearly as hard to catch as you might have thought they were.

CHAPTER 2

"Up-Country" Reds

Folks occasionally take great liberties with words and phrases, using them way out of context with their true meanings in order to get a point across. For instance, as two anglers set out for a day of fishing, one turns to the other and declares, "I'm going to kick your butt today!"

Now we're all pretty sure that the speaker has absolutely no intention of booting his partner in the behind. The phrase, through the mystical evolution of the English language, has somehow grown to mean that he intends to outdo his friend—in this case he feels he will catch more fish. In this application—if you are capable of somewhat loose interpretations—the phrase is not too difficult to understand, though for the life of me I cannot see how any form of music could be referred to as "kick-butt."

If you are a stickler for proper grammar and know a little about redfish, you may have some problems with the term used to describe the focus of this chapter, since it denotes *interior* land areas—where there is normally a notable paucity of redfish. Let's just say I used some literary liberties to create a kick-butt title. It got your attention, didn't it?

Although the title may not be scientifically or grammatically correct, it is descriptive in its implication: as summer waxes, redfish move farther and farther up-country from the sea, to the interior areas of many coastal marshes, even into locations known better for black bass and other freshwater species than for reds. There, they offer action which can often exceed that which is found in the brackish and salt marshes nearer the seashore. Experiencing such fishing, however, can require some fairly radical changes from the patterns normally productive in the "outer" areas.

No matter where it may be found, the "up-country" is a world apart from that in which most folks fish for reds. In many areas, cypress trees—and the stark remains of those of yesteryear—rise from the surface of the ponds. Elephant ears, rushes, and bull tongue line the shorelines; willows, hackberries, and tallow trees sprout from the ridges along creeks and canals, and morning glories grace the hummocks, often in a rainbow of colors.

Submergent aquatic grasses are usually profuse here, covering the bottoms of the ponds and frequently rising to the surface to form solid vegetative mats. In many such areas nutrias and muskrats graze innocently on these plants, alligators furtively stalk them and other prey through them, and ospreys dive gracefully onto surfacing mullet around its edges where—here and there—redfish crash noisily into schools of killifish, juvenile mullet, and pygmy sunfish. Up-country is indeed a place of beauty, a place to marvel, a place to lose your concentration on the business at hand. Distractions are everywhere—and you can grow not to mind that a bit!

Admittedly, it was a distraction that led to my first up-country red. At the time, I was bass fishing with fly-rod poppers from a paddlecraft in a canal. The gallinules were especially raucous and playful that early summer morning, and when I committed that first deadly sin of bass bugging—shifting my concentration from the popper to something else, in this case a very rowdy bird close at hand—a redfish stuck its tail out of the water squarely in my line of vision! An encounter with a red in that particular area being one of the farthest things from my mind, I did get a bit rattled, but I managed to flip the popper close enough to the fish to get its attention, and it struck on the second pop. At the time, it was the largest red I had ever caught from "inside" waters (those found inland from the seashore). After 35 years, it remains the largest (just under 15 pounds) that I have taken from up-country waters on a fly!

That brings up an interesting point. My fishing log indicates that with only one exception, every inside red I have caught that weighed 12 pounds or more was taken from a fresh, or almost fresh, marsh. And if that doesn't emphasize the potential of the up-country in terms of productivity, there was the fish an acquaintance caught not long ago in a quite shallow and almost-fresh marsh just up the road a ways from my erstwhile home in the Mississippi River Delta. It weighed—hold onto your hat now—$21\frac{1}{2}$ pounds, and, by the way, it was also caught on fly tackle.

There are two very good reasons why heavyweight reds are often found in the up-country. The first is that it holds a veritable profusion of numerous types of prey species. Besides killifish, stomach content analyses on fish taken from these waters (a ritual procedure conducted just prior to filleting them!) have revealed "mystery" fish, common eels, blue crabs, small mullet, and large white shrimp. I have no doubt that baby bass are also on the menu, as are the offspring of the redear sunfish I found bedding on a favorite redfish flat one summer. No kidding!

The other reason is that the lush aquatic vegetation provides excellent cover for a redfish looking for a meal. Whether he is tilted up and tailing with his nose in the goop as he searches for a crab, whether he is slowly cruising along the edge of a thick mat or grass island in an attempt to flush a school of minnows, or whether he is simply laid up in the salad waiting for something appetizing to swim by, he doesn't have to expend a lot of energy to eat. That in itself—efficient feeding"—leads to the production of big fish.

On the other hand, all that vegetation can present a formidable problem for the angler.

First, in many cases he must be able to make his way through and across it in his boat to reach the fish. Up-country reds are just as fond of skinny water as their cousins in more saline areas are. Here, though, the heavy vegetation in the shallow flats and ponds can prevent easy access by bass boats, bay boats, and the like, and a trolling motor will grass up so quickly that it is virtually worthless as a means of propulsion.

However, there are several solutions to the problems of gaining and traversing the shallows in these areas. One is to transport a paddlecraft—canoe or kayak—in the bigger boat. Upon reaching the area you intend to fish, anchor it in deep water, slide the smaller boat overboard, and use either a paddle or a push-pole to propel it.

Mud boats powered by air-cooled, straight-drive motors (i.e., GO-DEVILs) can be used to both gain and cross these areas. Nevertheless, for purposes of stealth they should be push-poled once the fishing has begun. The same goes with a shallow-draft, outboard-powered aluminum flatboat, though craft like that can also be paddled. Over the years I have used all three of these options with almost equal success, though I prefer using a secondary boat. Yes, it's a bit of a hassle, but occasionally I seem to do a little better fishing from it than from the larger craft.

One reason for that could be the result of another problem one faces when working these areas: the water's extreme clarity. All that submergent grass—which by midsummer has probably reached its full growth potential—serves as an excellent filter. Therefore, the water in the shallows here is often quite clear, allowing for excellent sight-fishing opportunities—and allowing excellent opportunities for the fish to see you first!

This creates a catch-22 situation. If you fish while standing—

and use a push-pole to maneuver the boat—you can see fish a lot farther from you than you can while seated and paddling. But in order to prevent them from detecting your presence, you must make fairly long casts, and in this setting, accurate casting is a must.

On the flip side of that coin, if you are seated you will not normally see as many fish, but those you do encounter will be less likely to notice you. Also, they will be closer, allowing shorter and thereby what should be more accurate casts. It's your choice; just understand the pros and cons of each method. Personally, I like to sit and paddle in "tight" marshes and small ponds and stand and push-pole across broad, open areas.

Small but "loud" surface lures can be excellent choices for up-country reds

Fish can appear literally anywhere around you. That factor demands you cover the water slowly, quietly, and thoroughly—"hunting" more than actually fishing. On days with bright sunlight and therefore the best subsurface visibility, you should not cast blindly as you move along; spot-casting to fish you see is by far the best tactic. The exception occurs on windy or dark days when reds that are not exhibiting sundry parts of their anatomy above the water's surface are next to impossible to detect. Then, you have no choice but to accept the inevitability of spooking occasional fish by either "lining" them or by the lure impacting the water too close to them while you're casting "speculatively."

We'll discuss that a little further in a moment. Now, let's assume that conditions are favorable for sight fishing, and as you make your way onto some promising shallows—in whatever type of appropriate boat and either sitting or standing—you are faced with the problem of where to begin looking for them. Do you remember I mentioned they could be anywhere? Well, that's true, but you would do best by ignoring those you will probably notice, which are randomly scattered about—provided they are not persistently waving their tails at you—and concentrate your search along "edges,"

Edges commonly occur as shorelines of emergent grass islands, the perimeters of interior ponds, and the rims of mats of submergent grasses. Downwind edges are best, as they create a narrow band of flat water before the ripples begin—a definite aid to spotting the indications of a red's presence. Look! One just tailed up against that patch of bulrushes over there!

Now you are faced with another problem. The fish is in no more than 10 inches of water and within a foot of the bank. You can't cast beyond it to draw the lure across its path, because you will likely foul the lure in the rushes. If you cast too close to the red you are guaranteed to spook it, and if you "lead" it too much it might turn away and never see the lure. Now what?

That exact situation is what initiated my 35-year career of fly fishing for up-country reds. Notably, it was done mostly with poppers, which floated above the submergent grass, seldom spooked fish when placed a couple of feet directly ahead of them, and provided an obvious target for them. Simply put, fly-rod poppers have proven to be unequivocally the best lures for reds found in this setting—for me, anyway.

That notwithstanding, I realize that many readers do not fish with flies. Fortunately, there are conventional techniques that can be successfully applied up-country.

The first is to thread a 36/40-count shrimp (which weighs a little less than half an ounce) onto a size 1/0 hook—no weight, no snaps or swivels, and certainly no float—lob it with a spinning outfit to a point about 3 feet ahead of the fish, and let it soak while you hope the red will detect it by smell. That has worked in the past, and it is quite exciting to watch the fish in its hunt for the shrimp!

Should you be averse to fishing with bait, another tactic that has also worked very well over the years is to thread a 3-inch, soft plastic grub—the curly-tailed types are especially good—onto a size 1/0 hook, leaving the point slightly buried in the lure, as you would do to render a plastic worm "weedless." Then cast it into the bulrushes slightly ahead of the fish, pull it gently into the water, and then work it across his path. (I've also done this—unintentionally, I admit—with flies and caught plenty of reds as a result, so the technique has several worthy applications.)

Finally, if there is no grass on the surface of the water along the bulrushes' edge, a small surface lure such as a Tiny Torpedo can lead to explosive entertainment. If possible, wait until the fish stops or tails up again, then make an easy lob cast to a point 2 or 3 feet ahead of him and let the lure sit. With the fish's nose on bottom, he will be less likely to spook from the lure's impact than he would otherwise. Then, when he stops tailing, begin a retrieve consisting of continuous short, soft twitches.

While the redfish you see around the islands and in the ponds often have a backstop of sorts behind them, making them difficult, albeit exciting, nuts to crack, those found along the edges of matted submergent grasses are often quite easy. If the mat is well defined—having little if any "stray" grass reaching the surface away from its perimeter—then a surface lure or a spinnerbait can be effective. Cast either type parallel to the fish's track so that the lure will pass him a couple of feet distant, and he will usually crash it. But here—as anywhere else in the grassy shallows where I am not faced with a "backstop"—my favorite lure (aside from fly-rod poppers) is a buzzbait. It is also the source of the best action on those cloudy or windy days, when the difficulty in spotting fish leads to the necessity of blind-casting. Incidentally, under these conditions buzzbaits can also lead to some fine supplementary action with bass, even in the shallows, even in the middle of a sultry summer afternoon!

That's just a little lagniappe (an unexpected bonus) and a part of fishing the up-country that makes it so appealing. My choice of buzzbait is a $\frac{3}{16}$-ounce Lunkerlure with the skirt removed and a "junior-sized" ($2\frac{1}{2}$-inch) paddle-tailed grub similar to a Sassy Shad attached. It gives me the distinct advantage of being able to cast across the fish's path—even if that means I must retrieve it across the top of the mat before it reaches the fish—without fouling. Well, sometimes. Remember, though, to never retrieve the lure directly toward the fish. The speed of the retrieve should be just fast enough to keep the lure on top. When one of those perch-stuffed heavyweight reds hits it, no one will have to tell you that you just had a bite.

Sadly, many up-country marshes have sorely degraded in recent years; some that once blessed the Mississippi River Delta are now entirely salty, others have completely vanished because of subsidence. Happily, though, many remain. They are wonderful places—aesthetically pleasing and full of wildlife wonders, and in summer redfish will join the bass and other freshwater creatures inhabiting them to provide some great action. Get yourself some of it; it's a kick-butt opportunity to the max!

CHAPTER 3

Oysters

O ysters are one of the most common forms of benthic structure found in redfish country. As such, they deserve a chapter of their own, not for biological purposes but to explain how their various forms of accumulation govern the best ways to fish for the reds that have been attracted to them. And here, since reds are often not all that's around, I am compelled to mention other creatures that just might strike a redfish-directed lure.

There's a fine line between folks who eat oysters like a big black drum and those who wouldn't touch one with their fingers! Personally, I love 'em, and not only on the half shell, fried, Bienville, in a soup (*not* a stew, which I feel is a waste of perfectly good oysters!), or in a dressing. You see, oysters create fish-attracting structure along much of the Gulf and Atlantic Coasts, and in many areas it's the best around.

Over the years, I have fished regularly over oysters and have determined three different forms of structure that are created from them: live reefs, cultivation beds, and the shells of dead ones. While all three can hold redfish—and specks (a.k.a. spotted seatrout), black drum, flounders, sheepshead, and more—at any given time and throughout much of the year, some consideration should be given to each type in order to achieve the best overall results.

Live Reefs

Live reefs typically present more vertical relief than the other forms of oyster structure, and they are less subject than the others to year-to-year changes. Those factors contribute to their appeal to the fish and to the relative ease of effectively fishing them.

Any accumulation of oysters provides both food and protection for several prey species. The larger such an accumulation is, the more likely it will attract prey, and large concentrations of prey are more attractive to predators than smaller ones. Therefore, of all types of oyster structure, live reefs are more likely— usually!—to hold large numbers of predators than cultivation beds or shell piles. However, in order to enjoy the potential that reefs offer, first you must locate one.

Over the years, I have occasionally accomplished that feat with relative ease, courtesy of my outboard's lower unit. It's an effective method in relatively shallow water, though it isn't too good for the health of your lower unit and is therefore not recommended as a standard, intentional practice! Still, just in case you do succeed in locating one in this manner, forget about it on that particular day, since you've assuredly run off any fish that were around. But mark its location, either on your GPS unit or by some nearby features, and be sure to return to it on your next trip—a little more cautiously, please.

A less extreme way to locate reefs is by noticing changes in the water's hue—oysters creating a darkness within a surrounding lighter bottom. Another way, especially for reefs in depths or clarity where they cannot be visually detected, is to drop a GPS waypoint on every spot where you encounter fish "randomly" in open water—especially specks running shrimp. Review those numbers from time to time, and if you discover that two or three of them are close together, the chances are good that you've found a reef—and a spot to prospect regularly even without the telltale signs of feeding specks!

Finally—and this applies to all oyster structure—a very low tide can be quite revealing. Scouting trips made at low tide, even though any actual fishing may not be all that good, can be excellent investments. Just be careful, since low tide is also a fine time for more than just polishing your prop!

Reefs are quite irregular, and their perimeters—and any high and low spots within them—are the primary strike zones. For reds (and specks!), these areas should be worked while on the trolling motor, and even if a concentration of fish is discovered, if at all possible do *not* set the anchor. Maintain position with your trolling motor.

Cultivation Beds

Beds for cultivating oysters are found in areas that support redfish, especially in Louisiana. These are primarily sections of bay bottom that are leased from the state and "planted" with seed oysters, which are gathered from public reefs and grow to marketable size in a year or so. Then they are harvested for sale by the leaseholder. Their perimeters are usually plainly marked with either long willow branches or lengths of PVC pipe, making them easy to locate. They can also change in character dramatically from year to year, and that makes them inconsistent producers at times. But man, when they're hot, they're hot!

Beds generally don't have the amount of vertical relief that characterizes reefs. Single oysters and small clusters are scattered randomly across the bottom, with accumulations in one particular

Where you find oysters, you'll find redfish, often big ones.

area often being much greater—and much more productive—than in others. In clear water, these oysters also show up as dark splotches on the bottom, but by the time you spot one, you've probably gotten so close that you've scattered any fish that had been present. The best way I've found to fish a bed is to drift across it with the breeze. If you must rely on trolling motor power, set it on the lowest speed that will get the job done, leave it alone, and if at all possible do not set the anchor. And since I've stressed that point twice, that's because anchors make a loud CLUNK! when they hit an oyster. And I'd imagine just about every reader knows what happens then.

The reason that beds are inconsistent is because of the work that is performed on them by the leaseholders. The hotspot you found last fall could easily be barren the following summer because the feature that made it hot has been altered in the meantime. Therefore there is no long-term justification for dropping waypoints on productive spots in a bed. Conversely, a spot in a bed that was a "dead zone" last fall could hold the mother lode next spring—again, the result of work having been done by the leaseholder. Cover a bed thoroughly and entirely!

On that note, beds are often created in relatively shallow water with slightly deeper channels within or alongside them.

These are avenues of sorts for both prey and predators and often hold reds and other gamefish in good numbers. Those that happen to be near the outside of the bed's perimeter can be plainly defined by the stakes that mark the bed. However, those that traverse the interior of the bed are not so easily determined and are often discovered at close range while fishing.

At that point, there is nothing you can do to convince any fish that were around and weren't scared out of their wits by the sudden presence of your boat to bite.

However, you assuredly *can* mark the place for future reference. Nearby stakes and crab trap buoys serve that purpose well, and when there aren't any around, you can always set your own. I have used crab trap buoys in the past with fine results, and the competition has no clue that they are not marking a crab trap but a prime piece of fishing structure. The only problem arises when the leaseholder comes along and picks them up in his dredges, but for a while after that happens the immediate area isn't usually very productive anyway.

Scattered Shells

Shells that remain from dearly departed oysters can be found both scattered and concentrated. One of the best ways to locate them in the latter form is to find an old fishing camp whose owner—past or present—regularly shucked his oysters from a particular spot on the porch or pier. Over the years, the shells beneath that spot can accumulate into a veritable calcareous mountain that often remains after all other signs of the camp are gone. In that instance, these shells can also be hazardous to your lower unit, but when there is some visible indication that they might be present—they create a color change, extend above the water's surface, or there are visible pilings and such that remain from the erstwhile camp—they can be easily and safely located. And they can draw fish, especially reds, like you would not believe! Oyster-eating camp owners of yesteryear have unknowingly provided me with more redfish, as well as a few lovely specks, than I would care to count.

Scattered shells are the least productive form of oyster structure, but they can provide good action. In clear water, these often appear rather randomly as both light and dark spots on bottom and have virtually no vertical relief. Nevertheless, in places they apparently serve to provide at least some food and protection for prey, especially in areas where the bottom is otherwise rather featureless.

A low tide also facilitates locating accumulations of scattered shells. Those are often given away by the presence of some that are then exposed along a presently dry or very shallow shoreline. Those shells that are visible at low tide can hold fish on higher water, but the "secret spot" is frequently in the deeper water just outside of them. Likewise, any shells you notice on the shoreline during periods of higher tides often indicate the presence of others off the bank a ways. These two scenarios will seldom lead to the discovery of a honey hole, but they could give up another red or two, or even a good speck or flounder for the cooler, trip after trip.

And speaking of the cooler, refrain from sampling the "structure" unless you are absolutely certain it is public and open for, well, sampling. There are more than enough palette-pleasing creatures commonly found on oyster structure for you to risk a problem in the tummy or otherwise with the shellfish. If you simply must have some, buy a sack on the way home—and a six-pack. They sure go well together!

That said, I have found that successfully working oysters—in any of the forms they are normally found—is best determined by the depth of the water they are found in. Generally, spinner-baits are the top all-round choice, but if the water is less than, say, 3 feet deep and clear and calm enough to allow their use, I simply cannot resist doing the Dog. In choppy or slightly turbid water of similar depths, a $\frac{1}{8}$-ounce jig-head dressed with a soft plastic grub and suspended beneath a popping cork a bit off the bottom can result in almost obscene action. Serve it at your discretion, either straight up or sweetened with a small shrimp.

One rather important note here. Since oysters tend to concentrate reds, that makes them great structure for prospecting with flies. Use fairly large poppers—size 1 or 1/0 and some 3 to $3\frac{1}{2}$ inches long—in the same scenario that is best for doing the Dog (fishing a Mirrolure Top Dog), though some folks I know from Texas who are blessed with exceedingly clear water tend to like much smaller poppers. Clouser Minnows suffice otherwise. And while this is usually a blind-casting opportunity, it can lead to action most fly-fishing folks can't even imagine, especially during winter, at least in some places along the Gulf Coast, such as the Mississippi River Delta.

Oysters in slightly deeper or really dirty water demand the use of jigs, $\frac{1}{4}$-ounce being a good choice. Again, serve them either straight up or sweetened, and work them slowly across bottom. If they hang up occasionally, that's good—you know you are in the strike zone. Just don't find yourself catching more oysters than redfish. You sure don't want to get tempted into sampling the structure!

CHAPTER 4

Changes for Good or Bad

I t is said that nothing ever stays the same. Well, I'm not so sure about that. The wind still whistles when the weather forecasters say it won't, the weeds continue to take over my backyard every February, and black Jack Daniel's tastes every bit as good today as it did 40 years ago. Speaking of black Jack, do you know it's only 80 proof now? Man, that's a change! Anyway, back on track now, when it comes to benthic structure, that which is of or occurring at the bottom of a body of water, it is oh so true. Take a certain little oyster bed I relied on for unfailing action over many, many years.

It is roughly the size and shape of a football field, and the water's depth throughout it is a relatively consistent 4 feet. Usually I would enter it through the south "end zone," and the fish are almost always found beyond the 50-yard line and within the right (east) half of the field. That's where I expected to find them on a trip there that had relevance to these lines. However, on that day (and on two subsequent days) there wasn't a red on the playing field! They were beyond the north end zone—totally outside the markers defining the bedding grounds—in an area I had often tried in the past, without any success whatsoever!

It was understandable that I could have blundered onto a stray school of fish one day, but not on three straight trips! That, along with the complete absence of them where they should have been, led to the realization that something had changed.

The obvious reason why the fish were no longer in their time-honored spot was that the oyster fisherman who owned that lease had dredged the bed since my last trip there, removing whatever it was that the fish had held to for so long—a scenario mentioned in Chapter 3 that is a common occurrence with this form of structure. Why, then, were they schooled up in the same spot outside the bed on three separate occasions? Who knows, but something fashionable must have certainly been there—a small hill or even an accumulation of oysters that had been inadvertently placed outside the staked area—that attracted and held the fish.

The point is, once again, that oysters are common along the coast, they create popular and productive structure, and that— like all forms of benthic structure—oyster structure is quite subject to change. It is very possible that one day you will discover that one of those long-time honey holes of yours is devoid of fish. When that occurs, don't lose heart—look around. The absence of what was once the primary structure in the area may cause the fish to be attracted to some form of "secondary" structure nearby.

One of the most notable instances I have witnessed of that happening was in the area surrounding Hell Hole #1—a derelict petroleum facility in one of the bays behind my once-upon-a-time home in Buras, Louisiana and once a redfish magnet of the first order. The reason for its productivity was that the bay bottom surrounding it was covered with odds and ends of oil field scrap iron, upon which grew oysters and provided neat cover for a plethora of prey creatures. The reason for its name was that it was therefore home to some very big fish, reds and specks alike, which, upon being hooked, would typically dive into the structure and almost always cut the line. Still, if after a hook-up you were quick to use the trolling motor to escape to safe water, if all your knots were tied correctly, and if your luck was running in the right direction, you could (occasionally) keep a red out of the structure—if it wasn't too big. Frequently it was.

Although the platform remained in place for some time after it ceased operating, a few years before its removal the owners cleaned all that wonderful junk off the bay bottom around it. One might assume that the platform itself would have still served to hold fish, but the only ones I encountered there during its final years of existence were sheepshead, small specks, and an occasional rat red. The big reds and the few big specks that inhabited the dangerous waters in which the platform once stood had long since scattered. However, a nearby oyster bed—where I had previously never caught enough to get a decent stink out of a skillet—shortly thereafter began producing numbers of very nice fish of both species! Look around—a cold hotspot can lead to a hot coldspot!

Good fish-attracting forms of benthic structure can be added to an area—at times, surprisingly quickly—as well as removed from it. Still, in order to locate them, one must be fairly familiar with the area.

I recall a trip to an early-season hotspot when I noticed that one of the previous winter's storms had blown away the remains of a fishing camp that had been around for many years. In its pre-storm condition it had been a consistent producer, though most often it gave up only a few fish at a time. Now only the pilings remained, and as a friend and I passed by it, I made a mental note that one day soon I should try to locate the rest of the camp.

A couple of weeks later, on another run to that early-season hotspot, we found the water dirty there, so we headed back to a clearer area and eventually decided to do some prospecting around the old camp. There—in one very specific spot on one side of it—we quickly caught almost 20 very nice specks. All right, so they weren't reds—they could have been! And they serve to illustrate this pattern very well, I hope. Anyway, jigs that were lost to snags well away from the pilings clearly indicated that the fish were holding over part of the camp that had been deposited on the bottom by the storm, and all the while we were catching them, we were joking about whether the fish were in the kitchen or the bedroom.

Besides oysters and manmade debris, benthic structure can be a natural phenomenon. One form that is relatively common in some areas is the result of coastal erosion: submerged flats, points, and humps that were marsh not long ago. To find these, it again helps greatly to have been familiar with the area before the loss took place, but it is not absolutely necessary.

For instance, a friend and I were fishing a small oyster bed along the edge of what had once been a large bay and what had become an even larger bay, and a very shallow one in the places where there had been marsh a few years back. A boat approached us, showed consideration by slowing to break his wake as he passed us some 100 yards distant, and then got up on the squat—not the "step"—and proceeded directly toward a long-submerged point, which he apparently didn't know existed. I casually mentioned to my friend that the ole boy wouldn't go much farther on that heading. He didn't.

Now I am certainly not recommending that you use your lower unit to locate this form of structure, any more than I did for locating oysters! Nevertheless, if you *accidentally* discover some of it that way—or better yet, if you notice the lighter hue the water takes on when it is shallow—and slow down to take a look before you run aground on it, then you may have found a promising spot. However, either way you will initially be faced with some considerations as to how and where to best fish it.

First of all, you should define the feature's perimeter, and I must say that by doing so you may spook every fish nearby. Sure, work the spot while you are learning it, but consider this an investment for future trips.

If there are oyster lease stakes in close proximity to the high spot, they can be used as easily recognizable reference points. If there aren't any, then use your compass and distant features—camps, treelines, grass islands, and the like—to establish the limits of the structure and the directions its edges follow. Let's use the ole boy who grounded his boat on the long-submerged point as an illustration of how to do it.

Just before he realized that the bottom had suddenly gotten awfully close to the top, he was in about 4 feet of water. At that particular tide—normal low rising with around a foot of range—the place where he hit bottom is about a foot deep. Once he fought his way back to the deeper water, he should have killed his outboard, dropped the trolling motor, and begun to make his way along the edge of the point, casting ahead of him to points along the drop-off if he so chose, but mainly establishing the direction in which the drop-off on that side of the point ran.

Following the drop-off, which is easily determined in those tidal conditions in reasonably clear water, he could then establish the limits of the point. If there were oyster lease stakes nearby (which there were on that side of the point), he could use them as references, i.e., the point's northern drop-off roughly parallels that line of stakes over there, lies about 30 feet south of them, and ends around 100 feet south of those two stakes that are planted in such a manner as they form a tight V.

Now he should cross the end of the point and locate and follow its southern drop-off, noting that it runs almost directly toward a small grass island. Here, he will discover that the water south of the point is only around 3 feet deep and appears to be a broad flat. Here and there, he might notice scattered clusters of shells and oysters on the bottom, too, and he should file that data for future reference on speck runs, should he be so inclined.

Benthic structure can change from time to time. Keeping aware of these changes can lead you to productive redfishing.

Finally, he would reach the base of the point where it merges into a broad and very shallow flat, formerly the marsh of which the point was a part. From there he could look back to the north, where he grounded his boat, and notice that the point is about 100 yards wide, runs about 200 yards east and west, and tapers to a width of about 50 yards at its end. Of course, if no oyster lease stakes had been present, then that determination would have been a tad more difficult. However, the GPS units that show your previous track can define such structure with pinpoint accuracy. Make use of this valuable aid. You will catch more reds because of it!

Okay, you have defined the extent of the point, hill, or whatever bottom structure you have discovered, and now you are on your next trip there. The water is again clear, the weather is nice with a light easterly breeze, and the tide is about the same as it was when you scouted your new-found spot. Now, where and how do you fish it? Let's use the point again as an illustration.

On normal tides, I will approach it at idle speed from the north toward its base. There I will kill and trim the outboard up a bit—not all the way, though, because of the lower unit's help in maintaining steerage, and use the trolling motor to move about halfway across the point. There I begin a drift with the easterly breeze along the point's length. Casts are directed toward the point's northern drop-off as well as across the shallows ahead of me. Although the reds can be just about anywhere on top of this old sweet spot, the edge of the drop-off is often the most productive area. And during the particular stage of the tide when I do much of my fishing here—normal low on the way to rising a foot or more—the same is basically true with all types of this form of structure. And I'll tell you this: if you work a high spot on the bay bottom like that one and don't use a surface lure, then shame on you!

There are two important points to remember here—well, besides not to ground your boat in your intended target area. The first, if at all possible, is to work it "fair-wind," which is the quietest way. If that allows you to cover the majority of the structure, so much the better. If it doesn't, then cover it by drifting in swaths, returning to your next starting point via a semicircle back through the water you have already covered, rather than in a fashion that requires constant trolling motor power.

The second point is the effect of a different tide on such structure. If it's below normal and you can still drift across, fish it—just make certain that the drift will not result in putting you in even shallower water. Conversely, on high tides, you'd best try to find some shallower water somewhere else, unless you can be satisfied with a mess of specks. If you're flexible, you'll eat better, I've always said!

Another way to find benthic structure that has resulted from subsidence is to prospect the waters around any "pipeline crossing" signs you may come across. These are fairly common in many areas along the coast, and you can bet your last spinnerbait that when they were erected, they stood on the shoreline of whatever body of water the pipeline crossed. Those you now see standing "out in the middle of the bay" are clear indications that the marsh once extended out to them, and the old drop-off from the grass into the bay should still be somewhere nearby. The tactics that apply to working the submerged points and hills are identical here.

Always approach a pipeline sign from the side that you are supposed to read. The deeper water will be on that side. Behind it will be the shallows, the erstwhile marsh. The drop-off—along which is the primary strike zone on normal tides—will probably be on an imaginary line roughly paralleling the plane of the sign. Find a spot like this—and there are plenty of them—and I'll guarantee that everyone who passes you will think you are a rank rookie, fishing "out in the middle of the bay," but I'll also guarantee you will often have the last laugh on them!

One last note. Many of those old shoreline drop-offs—no matter if they are the edges of submerged points, hills, or the once-upon-a-time banks near a pipeline sign—are not as steep as they were when they supported grass, having been eroded into gradual slopes by wave action. As such, they may not appear to be worthwhile structure. Don't you believe it! During low tide periods—say, the last quarter of the falling stage back up through the first quarter of the rising, and even during the slack times— reds will feed along them just as they did in the days when the grass was present there and the drop-offs were more sharply defined. That, at least, is one thing concerning benthic structure that has remained the same since I began fishing such stuff over 30 years ago.

CHAPTER 5

Puddling

A while back, I was invited to give a talk at the annual all-day conclave of a chapter of the Federation of Fly Fishers. I had presented programs at similar events and other gatherings, as well as at other chapters' monthly meetings for over a decade, and had gotten to know many of the folks fairly well. I was chatting with one of them when I noticed a large number of kayaks, canoes, and other forms of paddlecraft mounted atop some of the members' vehicles, and when I mentioned it, my friend said they were the craft of the "puddlers"—those who pursued redfish into very shallow water with them. Then he paused for a moment, looked at me as if he had just recognized me, and stated: "You know, you gave us a program about fly fishing for reds from a small boat at one of our group's first meetings—that makes you the original puddler!"

Well, I don't know about that. It was simply a very effective means that I had stumbled across for catching redfish, and not only with flies.

I was in a pirogue—the "Cajun canoe"—when I caught my first Louisiana red on a fly. That time, its purpose was not for coping with very shallow water, but for accessing an isolated section of a canal in some nearby up-country marsh. Earlier that year, the clear water therein had beckoned strongly, and I had used the pirogue—ferried there and back in my bass boat—to enter it. I quickly learned that the canal was full of bass—and caught the biggest speck I had ever taken anywhere—on a spinnerbait!

One lovely June morning shortly thereafter, I was working a small popper along the canal's overhung grass shorelines with an appropriately light outfit when the red waved its tail at me. It ate the little fly without hesitation, and after it had towed me up and down the canal for 20 minutes, or so I netted it aboard—and in the process came within a hair's breadth of capsizing the pirogue. That took place in 1971, and at just under 15 pounds, that red remains the largest I have caught on a fly in "inside waters."

Then there was the shallow-water advantage that the little boat offered, which manifested itself on a trip not long after the capture of the big red. Action in the canal had been slow, so I decided to prospect a big pond nearby. At that time, part of the pond could be accessed by bass boat through a small, meandering tidal cut between it and an open canal. However, an extensive flat along the pond's western side was too shallow for the bass boat. That day, from the pirogue, I got a pair of 8-pounders from that previously unattainable flat.

Bass boat access to the entire pond ended not long thereafter, when the open canal was re-dredged, plugging the cut with dredge spoils. On the few trips I made after that, I had to drag the pirogue across the spoil bank. This was no real problem, but the reds no longer seemed to like the pond as well as they once had, except for one, which was taken on a shrimp-sweetened popping rig. It weighed just under 16 pounds, and after almost 35 years it remains the largest "inshore" red I have caught on any type of tackle. Little boats open up an opportunity for big redfish.

As that famous old spot waned in productivity, another simi-

Canoes, kayaks, and other paddlecraft offer access to redfish in waters that are otherwise unreachable.

lar up-country marsh was rapidly becoming one of the finest I have ever known. It lay across a canal from which I hooked my first Louisiana redfish, on a spinnerbait, while I was walking along the canal's bank. During that fall, winter, and early spring I worked that and another canal that intersected the first one from my 11-foot wooden duck boat, catching a world of specks and a few smallish reds on jigs. Late spring and much of summer found me in my new bass boat prospecting some then well-defined "outside" waters. Then Hurricane Camille blew my wife Barbara and me north and kept us there while I finished my degree. We returned to the Delta in late January. There I again used the duck boat through the rest of winter and much of spring to catch some very nice reds—and a couple of rather huge ones—on spinnerbaits from another up-country canal.

That summer, I went to work for Gulf Oil Company as a lease operator in Black Bay, a large oil patch southeast of New Orleans at the edge of Breton Sound. The job consisted of five workdays and two days off—almost normal except for the 45-minute crew-boat ride to and from work. Normally we would get home around a quarter to five.

For the next year, my fishing continued to be done in the

outside bays from my bass boat and in a local canal from my duck boat, and soon from a newly acquired pirogue. That winter, I discovered the isolated section of the canal that yielded the big speck and later the outsized red, and the following spring I began to fully realize the value of the small boat for fishing for reds in the shallow marsh that I discovered near my home.

That area could not have been created any better for "puddling." Various emergent grasses throughout it grew tall enough to protect the small ponds within it from the effects of a moderate breeze. The bottom of the ponds was blanketed with widgeon grass that occasionally rose to the surface, forming protective mats for killifish, crabs, and shrimp, and prime hunting grounds for reds. Because of the grass, the water was as clear as tap water.

Fishing began immediately upon entering that marsh. A redfish tail could be waving enticingly, or the fish itself could appear quite plainly, against the protection of a grass shoreline, just around the next turn, just inside the next pond, or right against the next mat of widgeon grass. The only problem I could find with any of it was that I didn't have enough time to fish it during the afternoons after work.

But where there's a will, there's often a way. In this case, it was by the grace of Hal, a seaplane pilot who had a piece of property against the canal where I had been launching my pirogue in order to gain the marsh. He put a small building on the property and constructed a ramp for his seaplane on the edge of the canal nearby—and he let me keep my pirogue by the ramp. Talk about expediting matters—a 10-minute drive from the house, a minute or two to load and launch the boat, and five minutes later I'd be fishing.

On most after-work days, two or three fish would be the rule, though on my days off I often caught many more. Most were in the 4- to 8-pound class; several were in double digits, and one came close to the weight of the canal red.

That one was tailing contentedly in the center of a small pond when I first saw it. The pond was almost totally enclosed and could not have covered more than a quarter of an acre, so I had to be really stealthy as I approached the fish, stopped a short cast away, and gently set the anchor. A few moments later, the red showed its direction, and then, like so many of its kin that inhabited that marsh, it immediately ate a popper.

And then you should have seen the mud and the crud fly as it tore around that little pond, turning it into a mini-maelstrom. Apparently the fish couldn't find the escape route, so it kept going around and around it, spinning my pirogue on its tether like a child's top. I almost got dizzy! At just over 14 pounds, that was an awfully big red to have been in such a small pond.

But it wasn't nearly as big as the gar I mistakenly cast a popper at from a canoe some years later, had it strike, and then had it almost capsize me as it shot underneath the boat. Still don't know whether it was attacking me or just trying to escape its recent inconvenience. Either way, if you put a 6-foot alligator gar between a canoe and the bottom, which is (maybe) a foot beneath the boat, there's not much room left. I don't cast poppers at skinny-water alligator gar anymore.

Sadly, autumn of 1974 signaled the end of my fishing in that lovely patch of up-country marsh. A hurricane buffer zone was created throughout it by filling it in with sand and silt dredged from the river. My puddling efforts became a little more labor-intensive after that, though I still frequently used the pirogue, then a canoe—both ferried by a larger boat—for pursuing reds in the marshes down the river where I had taken the big speck and reds. That was also a fine area, and it held its grass—both emergent and submergent—very well until a decade of successive poundings by some serious hurricanes tore it all up. For what it's worth, there are still some reds there, but the water hasn't been as clear as it once was. I guess everything is bound to change. I was graced to have had it all as it was for so many years.

But there are still similar places along the southeastern coast—and others that are perhaps not quite so pretty but equally as productive—that are within a short paddle of a spot where you can safely park your vehicle. "Puddling" can open the doors to a lot of fine redfishing. So while I do not intend to delve into the particulars of the various types of paddlecraft that are suitable for pursuing redfish in shallow water, I will offer you some thoughts on associated matters.

Choosing a Paddlecraft

Consider the weight of the boat against its draft and how much weight it will normally be carrying. Lighter weight usually is better—shallower draft is always better!

Keep it under 12 or 13 feet long. If you discover you have need for anything larger, then you shouldn't be using one in the first place.

Carry two paddles with you—a long one (metal or whatever) for getting from here to over yonder, and a shorter wooden one for fishing once you get there.

Carry a small (3-pound) anchor on about 6 feet of nylon rope, and keep the rope tied to a thwart or seat.

If you choose a canoe, fish while sitting on an ice chest placed a close to amidships than sitting on one of the seats. This will help keep the bow down and therefore less subject to blowing around in the breeze.

Wear a life jacket while paddling from here to over there a ways. The inflatable types are not cumbersome and not too hot during the more temperate months. You can always take it off once you begin fishing—in the shallows!

If you intend to use a paddlecraft for fly fishing, wear slip-on tennis shoes or something similar, with no laces that can easily foul the loose fly line that will be around your feet while you are sitting.

Sitting lessens the ability to see into the water at a distance, but the stealth it provides offsets the difference. Redfishing from a paddlecraft in the shallow marsh should be just like hunting—make it so!

Finally, buy a new pickup truck. Seriously, you can get a pretty nice one for what a big new four-stroke outboard would cost. You are likely to catch more fish from a paddlecraft than you will from that bay boat you've got—well, maybe not, but close—and the truck will make loading and unloading it much easier than cartopping. That will save your back and prevent possible problems there down the way. See, there's all sorts of ways to justify it!

But whatever you do, consider puddling. It's a technique that can't be beat for fishing in an area where reds spend much of their lives.

The Seashore
and Beyond

CHAPTER 6

The Role of the Oil Field

In areas where it is present, oil field structure is one of the best redfish attractors and accumulators imaginable. I am something of an authority on that topic, having spent a very rewarding 25-year career in the south Louisiana oil patch, both inshore and offshore. And, at times, I was prone to fishing on the job.

I've caught reds (both on and off the job) around oil field structure in depths from a bit under 2 feet to almost 150 and ranging in size from rats less than a foot long to brawny bulls well over 30 pounds. I have also caught them in such habitat year-round and occasionally in such numbers that it bordered on being immoral—though certainly not illegal! Simply put, if the oil field fishery doesn't exist in your waters, I really do feel sorry for you.

Anyway, coastal oil fields can be divided into two categories: inshore and offshore. Since the inshore types occur in great part near the seashore, that is why this discussion is included in this section of the book.

In most cases, reds will be found close to (or even within) these structures and *on bottom*. That can range between roughly 3 and 15 feet or more deep, and the combination thereof usually requires presenting your enticers with some accuracy as well as with a good degree of feel—sort of like fishing deep in coastal river current. So here jigs are the recommended choice of lures, sweetened if the water is a bit grungy, straight up if it isn't. Fish them on at least 2 feet of 30-pound fluorocarbon leader and even then, be prepared to lose some of them to both fish and structure.

Losing reds in such "dangerous" water is simply part of the exercise, though I once tried to determine if "flipping"—a freshwater technique—would lessen those losses. It didn't, but I'll tell you this: the results of slamming the hook into a 6-pound red that's only a few feet away from you can be quite entertaining. If you feel that your redfishing has become somewhat tame lately, then try short-range flipping for them around some inshore oil field structure. But don't even think about doing this with your regular gear or you will assuredly be shopping for replacement tackle shortly thereafter. A heavy 7- or $7\frac{1}{2}$-foot "flipping stick," 30-pound mono, and the reel's drag screwed down to "stop" is required. So you think that sort of gear isn't "sporting"? Try it and see!

While flipping is indeed an exciting and productive method of fishing for reds around oil field structures, a moderate chop will generate hull slaps that will render it completely ineffective. When that rather common occurrence arises, you must work the structure from a distance in order to prevent the noise from spooking the fish, but that distance should be as short as possible to facilitate accurate casting and having at least some control over hooked fish. That is best accomplished by working the structure in the direction that creates the least amount of hull noise. Think about that before you begin prospecting one.

Anchoring the boat in order to work a particular part of the structure is not usually advisable. Stay on the trolling motor, and if a hooked fish makes a dash away from the line-shredding pilings, junk, and whatever else is around, then follow it quickly into safe water—and then do your utmost to keep it there. Admittedly, that can be rather difficult once a fish has reached double digits, but that's when it really gets fun!

And about that size. Throughout most of the year, my largest inshore reds have almost always been taken from oil field structures. Besides offering these fish a degree of cover, they draw and hold a variety of prey. In other words, they create a microcosm of sorts for reds, providing virtually everything the fish require.

And that can result from structures much smaller than even the smallest processing facility. I recall a particular gas well that was supplemented with a small platform that supported some drying equipment. The platform, around 10 x 20 feet, was constructed perhaps 50 feet from the well, and both were situated along the edge of a narrow but relatively deep access channel. Reds regularly held to the little platform near the channel's drop-off.

Or, in that case, maybe that wasn't quite correct, as the fish may have been holding to the channel's drop-off near the little platform. There is a difference. Various drilling and producing equipment, as good as it is, is not the only form of fish-holding structure that the oil field creates. Access routes to particular areas—and anything "different" in them, such as dead-end offshoots and intersections and even breakwaters that shelter critical docking facilities—can all hold fish. In other words, anything that would not be in the interior waters all along the coast had it not been for the oil field can, and often does, hold redfish.

In recent years, much of the best of the inshore oil field's "old iron" has been removed, and with it have gone quite a number of erstwhile hotspots. Also, the recent hurricanes wrecked others to the point where they must also be removed. Simply put, there are a lot fewer of these redfish magnets around these days than there once were.

But in areas where they have historically been present, there are usually still some! Keep a lookout for them—the older and junkier, the better! One of them just might give up some of the best redfishing you have ever experienced.

Offshore

"Offshore" oil-field platforms can also hold reds, occasionally in numbers that are difficult to believe. These often rather huge structures can be found from just beyond the seashore out to depths where a red wouldn't be caught dead, but those in water roughly 20 to 60 feet deep are quite acceptable to them. Not so incidentally, fish caught around those standing in state waters can be kept for the table—in accordance with the individual state's size and possession restrictions, of course—but reds caught in federal waters (the Exclusive Economic Zone, or EEZ) cannot legally be in your possession.

In either case, sweetened jigs are usually best and should be worked with slow, easy pumps near bottom. In the deeper water, a fish-finder rig finished with a size 8/0 circle hook impaled in a good-sized chunk of mullet or pogy (menhaden) is best, because the current masks bites, and a typical J-hook (as opposed to the circle hook) might be swallowed to the point where its removal could be hazardous to a fish's health. Bull reds are common around these platforms, especially those near shore, and you can wear yourself out playing catch-and-release with them. Handle with care, though!

And one note on that. No matter how well you handle them, reds caught in water more than, say, 50 feet deep will be subject to the "bends" (actually overinflated swim bladders) after being caught, and most folks simply do not know how to relieve a red of that possibly fatal problem. If you get into a school of reds around a platform in water that deep or greater, leave and go elsewhere!

Reds, especially bulls, can occasionally be found in large schools on the surface running sardines, menhaden, and the like. They also tend to feed with blue runners on the surface—or perhaps the "hardtails" tend to feed with them. Either way, if you come across a school of these small jacks, stop to take a quick look around. If any reds are present, you'll find out soon enough.

Contrary to the relationship between bulls and blue runners, little tunny (erroneously referred to as "bonito" in some areas), which also frequently feed on the surface in waters inhabited by reds, are not nearly as compatible. I assume that this is because the tunny are quite speedy in their pursuit of prey, and the reds simply can't keep up. In any case, don't waste time chasing little tunny in search of bull reds.

Still, keep a watchful eye out. The first bull red I ever caught on a fly was taken on the surface in offshore waters, from a school big and hungry enough to allow two other fish to be caught on flies by my companions as we drifted along with them. There were so many of them that the hooked fish wrecked my fly line by dragging it across the backs of others. Nevertheless, I surely couldn't complain. Find a school like it, and I'll guarantee you won't either.

The Hell Holes

I have mentioned one of these famous old sweet spots earlier in these pages. They both deserve more, and I intend to give it to them. You may not learn a whole lot about redfishing from what follows, but you might get a kick out of reading about it. For sure, it belongs.

So here's to all those talented and capable anglers—including yours truly—who, time and again, got ate slap up by reds while fishing for them in the dangerous waters that surrounded these two rather innocent-looking pieces of structure.

It sure was fun.

By the mid-1980s, the combination of rampant gillnetting and the loss of thousands of acres of spartina grass in what was then the "marsh" near my old home in the Mississippi River Delta often made for very difficult redfishing. Out of necessity alone, I eventually began prospecting derelict oil-field equipment, some of it quite small, which then littered the area and thwarted the netters, as well as providing structure the fish could associate with without being overly bothered. Two of the best of those places became fondly known as "The Hell Holes."

Almost two decades have passed since that day of particular enlightenment, but I remember the events almost as clearly as if they had occurred yesterday. The bright, early summer morning was made for sight-fishing—clear, calm, and not quite hot. But the enthusiasm that had built within me by the time I pulled away from the marina began to fade rapidly after I arrived at a favorite flat and discovered a gillnet stretched across it. A second spot was cursed with the same plight, and two boatloads of commercial guys were just leaving the third as I pulled up to it, their webbing woven across the shallows in such a manner as to render it completely unfishable. Back then, when someone was confronted with such atrocities, all he could do (legally) was to grit his teeth and silently curse those who were allowing so few the right to take so much at the expense of so many.

For a long moment, I just sat there in my skiff, wondering if there was any way I could reap a few ice-chest benefits from such a fine day. And then I noticed the small petroleum facility a short distance across the bay.

At the time, I had caught a few reds around such structures, though those had been much larger and in much broader bays than the one that had just tweaked my curiosity. However, the thought arose that the waters around it just might be considered un-nettable and might hold a few fish. Notably, two more boat-loads of commercial guys were in the process of setting their instruments of wreak and ruin along a nearby stretch of marshy shoreline—but they maintained a respectful distance from the structure.

I approached the facility slowly on the trolling motor and on the way noticed that the piping around it was badly corroded—some of it had actually rusted in two and fallen into the water. Plenty of snag potential here, I thought, as I lobbed my jig to a point between two of the platform's pilings, allowed the lure to sink a bit, and then began a slow retrieve with easy pumps—and almost immediately felt resistance.

"Snag" was my first reaction, but then a couple of violent head shakes proved me wrong. For some unknown reason, the fish decided to make its bid for freedom in open water rather than dive into the structure's pilings, and a while later I netted a red that, at almost 11 pounds, was larger than any other I had taken so far that year. But not for long! By working the perimeter of that rather small, rundown production facility—and by sticking my bent rod's tip into the water whenever the nearby commercial guys seemed to be taking an interest in the goings-on there—I caught well over a dozen more beautiful reds, one of which was larger than the first. Incidentally, I noticed the nearby philistines caught very little in their nets. Do you think I was one smug puppy!

On that quite memorable morning, a pattern was formed that has since led to some outstanding redfishing throughout all seasons of the year and often at times when the competition was having some difficulty catching enough to stink up their ice chests. Oil field-related odds and ends are perhaps the best form of inshore redfish structure along our coast, and it ain't too shabby offshore. The best of it is iron, and the best of that is old.

The aforementioned production facility is a prime example. Fact is, there was so much corroded iron lying on the bay bottom around it—most of which was covered with oysters—that the reds, especially the bigger ones, had little trouble cutting a line on it. Because of that, the place became fondly known as Hell Hole Number One, and those friends whom I introduced it to quickly learned why.

But man, the fish—and the wicked fun—that it produced!

The first such incident took place with a devout light-tackle spin fisherman. I had just caught a nice one with my rather stout casting outfit and 17-pound line, which at times was itself insufficient to turn a red away from the trash, and suggested he cast at a spot where a

Oil field structure can provide some of the best redfish opportunities imaginable.

short, piling-supported walkway connected two small platforms. He did, his cork soon dove, his little reel squealed as the fish neatly dragged his line against a piling, and that was that.

He paused for a moment, looked at me just as I burst out laughing, and mumbled, "I think I was just set up."

By the time a couple of years had passed, I had learned all the places around HH#1 where I should not cast. One of them seemed to always hold a big red, but because of the structure creating it, all the advantages were with the fish.

Two magazine editors from Atlanta came down one autumn for a picture-taking fishing trip. After putting them on some nice specks and fair reds early on, I decided to see if we could get a big red at HH#1. On the way, I developed an urge to set one of 'em up.

I pointed at the spot: "Cast right there."

The cast was well short.

"You have to get it close to the structure," I offered.

Short again.

"Bump the stump," I pleaded.

Short again, and I could stand it no longer. "No, like this!"

You guessed it. The cork hit the strike zone, I gave it one pop, it immediately disappeared, and very shortly thereafter you could chalk up one more for the adversary. I guess I deserved that one, but I never was able to get a fish out of that spot.

But we sure got a lot of them from its less dangerous waters!

Then there was Hell Hole Number Two—a similar accumulation of oil field rubble, though a little less dangerous, across the bay from Number One. The bottom of the bay that surrounded it was also littered with junk, though much of it was larger and more easily avoided. But line-shredding oysters grew on it in profusion, and drew the bait, which drew the fish.

A one-time supervisor of mine got a 2-foot speck one lovely spring morning at #2—the biggest he had ever caught. Some years later, in a breaking nor'wester between Christmas and New Years Day, the wife of a pine-cone-kicking buddy from north Mississippi got another 2-footer from the same place—also her largest. I thought her face would crack from the grin she wore for the rest of the day!

My daughter Christi passed a particular summer afternoon with me around #2, pitching spinnerbaits for reds. I got one that we weighed at just over 11 pounds, then revived and released it—and got a rousing ovation from a crew of nearby oil field hands who had been watching all along. That was a real ego trip, strutting my stuff in front of my daughter and then getting applauded for it. You don't forget things like that.

Then there was the one I caught on a spinnerbait one day at #1 with old Bruce that pegged the 12-pound scales. It's a good thing that fish had miscalculated its heading slightly, or I'd have never kept it out of the structure! There were a lot of big fish holding to those two spots, and every one that we somehow boated—and usually released—was a real accomplishment. And it was a heck of a lot of fun getting there!

Toward the end of the century, the owners of the Hell Holes decided to clean up around #1. Suddenly the little structure was stacked with all kinds of rusted, twisted, shell-encrusted piping that had been dredged from the bay's bottom around it, and that was the end of the great fishing there. A couple of years later the structure itself was removed, and with the continuation of the degradation of the local marsh, fishing got just a little tougher.

HH#2 suffered a comparable fate, though not quite as extreme. By the time my fly-fishing buddy Bubby and I began to hit it regularly on friendly winter days, the sparse "island" of Roseau canes around which the junk and oysters were scattered had shrunk to a fraction of its onetime size, and a lot of nearby "house-cleaning" had taken place. Still, on reasonably warm days with a hard-rising tide, we would often hit 'em hard—nice ones, too, even on flies.

My pine-cone-kicking buddies and I found them there again one late autumn morning not long ago, right where they were supposed to be. We caught them on topwaters and by popping plastics, and once again, they were all very nice fish. And we never broke off the first one on structure. HH#2 had lost a lot of its personality, even though it still attracted fish.

The following winter, I checked it out again. The canes were completely gone, as were the jumbled pilings and bits and pieces of the junk that remained and showed above the water's surface at low tide. But a few familiar markers around the spot remained, so I don't believe I'll have any trouble finding it again. Still, it's sad that another fine spot is threatened if not now extinct.

THE ROLE OF THE OIL FIELD

I'll best remember #1 as a spring and summer spot with big fish that were quite willing to help me set up a friend for a good laugh or two. I'll best remember #2 as a winter spot where on those delightfully crisp, cool afternoons Bubby and I put some serious hurting on 'em while everyone else afloat was suffering through the drudgery of fishing the deep holes down the road a ways. But I'll best remember them both as oil field junk piles that created two superb little fishing spots during a time when those were getting scarce in that area, and the fact that they were once somewhat "dangerous" only enhance their worth.

Yeah, I guess in the overall scheme of things their removal was best; they had done their time and served their purpose— and they had claimed far too much of my tackle. But that sure won't stop me from missing them.

CHAPTER 7

The Surf

Throughout the redfish's range, there are numerous places where anglers can access and fish the surf from the beach. A lot of different opportunities await them there, one of the best and most consistent being offered by the hero of these pages. Indeed, part of my education about reds that was really enlightening was the fact that in some areas, these fish are the source of some great action in the surf even in midwinter.

Also, with a few noteworthy exceptions—large coastal bays and sounds being foremost among them—nearshore waters are among the best places to encounter the largest of the species, the "bulls." These prize specimens often move from their offshore grounds to the various forms of structure found near beaches to feed and to spawn from roughly midsummer well into autumn— and, as I just mentioned, for considerably longer in some places. In many areas, bull reds become quite accessible to shorebound anglers during those periods. Indeed, some of the largest of the beasts are typically taken every year by boatless folks fishing such waters. The first to be covered here is the natural surf.

Initially, one must be aware of the sections of surf to fish on a rising tide, those that are best when it's falling, and those that almost never produce anything at any phase of the tide. This is especially important during summer, when many of these spots can also be inhabited by lifeforms other than anglers and redfish.

There, a considerable number of beings in bikinis and boxers and carrying boom boxes and beer coolers can begin to collect along the beach and breakers around midmorning, remaining there until suppertime. In the meanwhile, no matter what the tide is doing, there can be few places along that particular beach—and any like it—where a hungry red wouldn't be in dire straits of being stepped on and where someone could cast a jig or fish-finder rig without serious danger of planting it in human flesh! Throughout the beach-bunny season, such a section of shoreline is not worth prospecting.

The period from suppertime to dark is reputed to be much better for fishing during summer. However, for reds, anyway, I must disagree, usually finding the water uncomfortably hot and probably oxygen-poor at that time. Assuredly, I have caught a few suppertime reds—mostly bulls—in the surf at this time, but all of them were from an area that was too remote to be inhabited by beach bunnies. During the summer, better action usually occurs after dark.

Better still comes in early morning, and the best action of all comes in places and at times that are not normally beach-bunny habitat. And I must repeat: some of the best fishing in seaside waters—in all but the more northerly locales where redfish are found—comes in fall and winter. Better yet, the lures and techniques that are productive during the warm months are often equally so when chest waders and wool shirts may not be required, but they sure do feel good!

In many areas, the natural surf zone is made up of a sequence of a gradually deepening trough against the beach, a shallow bar roughly paralleling the beach, another trough, another bar, and then a progressively deepening descent into offshore waters. In

Fishing the surf can be a productive way to target redfish.

such an area, you normally won't find many fish. However, there are places along at least the Gulf Coast where, during late fall through winter, you can actually stand on dry land and catch reds until you are beat to the bone from the crystalline water that the season creates in the first trough. But that aside, more consistently good action—and the largest fish—usually come from the second trough.

In any case, unconformities within that sequence can serve to attract and concentrate the fish, or so this oil field taught me. But before we get into that, we must be able to define just what's a trough and what's a bar! There are two easy ways to make this determination. Deeper water (the toughs) is darker than shallower water, and waves break against the bars and glide across the troughs. Remember that!

Okay, bars with current-scoured, abrupt drop-offs—unlike the much more common types with rather gradual grades—are good prospects. So are cuts through the bars, especially the second one, that allow prey and predator access into the second trough—again, in my experience, the primary strike zone. On that note, though, some readers may disagree. Fine, but whatever the case, cuts through a bar are prime structure!

So are any places where a trough shallows and perhaps ends because of a "point" that extends from the beach through it and continues offshore a ways, disrupting the sequence. Where that occurs, it creates a trap the likes of which I am certain a redfish would just love to see more of. I sure would! Anyway, a spot like that can be easily detected by either the color of the water in the trough suddenly changing from dark to light, or by waves breaking against the edge of the submerged point. Work these spots either from atop the point or the first bar and far enough from the end of the trough to prevent spooking any fish that are within it.

Generally, these forms of surfside structure have proven to be best on a rising tide; however, I am a firm believer in fishing whenever you can—depending, of course, on whether sea conditions allow it. And that brings up a fine point. A rowdy surf is preferred by many anglers who fish while in direct contact with the earth. That condition stirs up the bottom sediments, which in turn inspires certain forms of prey to move about, and that inspires the redfish to feed, especially when it occurs at night. In such conditions, the odds of hooking a big one become pretty good. Use a fish-finder rig with a pyramid or other sand-grabbing type of sinker *that will hold bottom* in the current created by the waves, a size 8/0 or thereabouts circle hook, and the head of a large mullet.

Yeah, the head!

While after-dark fishing from the beach is popular in some places, probing much less severe waters in the comfort of a boat is preferred in others. This frequently takes place in a pass where one might think that the best times to fish would be on the falling tide, since that would draw prey from interior areas into the realm of the beachside bulls.

And indeed it does, but during summer and fall gangs of reds can congregate at the mouths of passes to spawn—on the rising tide! And all of them don't spawn at the same time. Those that momentarily aren't so inclined, eat. So during the falling tide, find a spot to anchor on the edge of the main current—that way you won't do too much rocking and rolling. During a rising tide, it is often possible to anchor comfortably anywhere you choose. In either case, soak your mullet heads on bottom, and be patient; action in a pass can go from dead stop to wide-ass open in seconds and at virtually any time!

There is one other form of structure that is found in these waters, especially along barrier islands or narrow strips of "land-based" seashore that separate inshore waters from the ocean. Both of those land masses have "backsides" that can, when the surf is a bit too rowdy for you pleasure, offer great fishing.

Those are most frequently marshy areas, and any cuts leading from them into the backside waters are the target area. They are invariably best on the falling tide, and while bulls may make rather rare appearances there, the numbers of "regular" reds can be more than enough to please even the greediest action seeker. Fish for them with quarter-ounce jigs or spoons, and if a gang of specks or a profusion of flounders—especially during autumn—precludes your action with the spot-tailed beasts, don't bitch about it! You can always hit the reds a lick once the tide starts to rise.

Sandbar Strategies

Sandbars are common across the coast, in estuaries as well as in the surf. They tend to be fairly dynamic, shifting, building, then washing away only to soon begin the cycle again. That's a means, incidentally, which can lead to a sudden disruptive and quite embarrassing end as you solidly ground your boat out in the middle of what had been deep enough water only a short while back. (Been there, done that *twice* recently!). But in their ever-changing role as a threat to your outboard's lower unit, wherever sandbars are found they are a prime form of redfish structure. For instance . . .

Late winter to very early spring was once a favorite time for some of my buddies and me to make our first annual trips out to some local barrier islands. We had to pick our days closely, wanting neither to meet an approaching norther head-on nor to get caught in a thick bank of sea fog, and we usually had to wear waders to ward off the water's chill. But with all that, the fishing could be quite good during that time, and generally we had the place to ourselves. On the first trip we made a few years back, my friends immediately set off to work the troughs and bars in the island's surf while I chose to explore its backside flats.

The flats on the backsides of that chain of islands are fairly featureless except for an occasional trough. Usually the fish are found in one of those troughs or not at all, and on that particular day, winter storms—or the lack of them—had caused one that had been particularly productive during the past season to fill in. I waded the entire length of the island without a strike.

As I approached its northern end, I noticed some small waves breaking almost 100 yards from shore; a sandbar had built there during the past months, and the perimeters of such submerged "points" are always worthwhile targets. While wading toward it, I noticed a large pocket of darker water between the lighter-hued shallows that I was crossing and the bar—very inviting! Upon entering the pocket to a point about thigh-deep I almost collided with a big jackfish (a.k.a. jack crevalle), and on my first cast I caught a fine redfish—the first of 13. Three of them were undoubtedly double-digit fish and, incidentally, all were taken on flies. I just *had* to mention that!

That particular point was not typical of the sandbars normally found at barrier islands, which tend to appear either within the trough-bar-trough sequence in the surf or as submerged longitudinal continuations of the islands. This one extended directly outward from the island's backside, and whether or not it was created from storm-scoured sand that resulted in the deep pocket adjacent to it is not important. What is important is the fact that sandbar "points" like this serve as blocking elements to baitfish being pursued by predators, and if there happens to be a deep pocket alongside one of them, that just enhances its potential.

Another type of point is found in the surf of both barrier islands and from mainland beaches. It was described briefly in the first section of this chapter and, I believe, warrants an anecdote.

On another early spring trip to that same barrier island (fact is, it was just after the trip just mentioned), I started out by working the pocket of deep water by the big backside point and didn't get a sniff. My friends had moved out onto the point itself and caught a couple of reds off its tip, then the action stopped. We soon split up and began to prospect.

After walking back to the island's south point and fruitlessly working a deep seaside pocket there, I began to make my way up the surf line. It was a drop-dead gorgeous morning—bright sky, clear water, and as calm as it gets, and the tide was just beginning to rise. About midway up the island, I saw a few pelicans diving near some small breakers extending offshore a short distance from the first bar: another submerged point. As I approached it I noticed that a couple of my buddies who were standing on the point were hooked up; then I detected a deep pocket on the near side of the point, which, it turned out, held no fish. By the time I reached my friends, the pelicans had dispersed, but I learned they had been diving into a big school of feeding reds. Well, if they were feeding then they should not have moved offshore, and they certainly had not moved into the pocket that I had just waded through. So I waded over to the first bar again and continued on up the surf. And it wasn't long before here came a pair of redfish, plainly visible in water less than knee-deep on *top* of the bar!

What ensued was both gleeful and slightly frustrating. I'd hook a red from a passing group, then as I had the fish close at

When surf fishing, seek out sandbars, which frequently attract and hold sizable reds.

hand, here would come another pair or so. They would flush from the commotion, then I'd release the fish, simply stand there looking—again, on top of the bar!—and it wouldn't be long before another small school would appear. Then the cycle was repeated, and I'll tell you this: catching them was surely fun— especially so since I was again fly fishing, but watching all those others pass by me while I was wrestling with another one became pretty hard to take after a while!

That was the first time I had ever encountered reds on top of the surf's first bar—and the progression of them along that bar was unlike anything I had ever witnessed in the surf. Notably, I did not see any fish in the first trough, though the angle of the sun made it impossible to see if any were passing me in the second trough. I have no idea why this event occurred, but the same pattern developed one morning a year or so later in the surf of another island. Take heed—reds *will* cruise the tops of the surf-side bars!

THE SEASHORE AND BEYOND

The submerged points that can occur on the ends of barrier islands are common features and are also top-notch structure. Here, an abrupt drop-off into deeper water on the offshore side of the bar occurs fairly frequently, and occasionally you will also find abruptly deeper water on its backside.

In that latter case one might assume the direction of tidal flow would have some bearing on which side of the bar is better to fish. However, past experiences have shown that no matter whether the tide was rising or falling, the fish should be found on the offshore side of the bar. Sure, speculate a few casts into any deeper water close to its backside, but don't waste a lot of time if strikes don't come quickly.

Also, don't initially wade far into deeper water that is immediately adjacent to any bar. I said it before and I'll say it again: either work it knee-deep or thereabouts along its edges or from the top of the bar itself. In the first case, take an occasional glance around you to see if any redfish have moved into shallower water. Frequently they will, especially on the rising tide, and they will go unnoticed if you aren't aware of that possibility. Or unless one swims up to you from behind and scares the bejesus out of you!

I've caught quite a few reds that were on top of the bars at the ends of an island. I have also not caught numerous others that had approached me quite closely, yet all I saw of them were big clouds of sand as they hastily departed after my presence spooked 'em! So while most of the reds you will catch here will be from the deeper water seaside—and it doesn't have to be all that deep!—keep an eye on the water around you.

On days when the surf is low and clear and the sun is bright and high in the sky—especially during the cool months—your position on top of any of the bars serves as an excellent vantage point for spotting fish in the nearby deeper water as well as in the shallows. I fondly recall standing on a favorite "south-point" bar early one delightful November afternoon with a dear old friend and watching two bulls swim by me, giving me two fine shots with a fly—both of which I bungled royally! That aside, sight-fishing in this setting is always a possibility. Just remember that they can probably see you, too, and they tend to cruise right along the drop-off a lot more often than they do atop the bar itself, so if at all possible, stand a short distance—15 feet or so—back from the edge of it while you are fishing.

A problem that sometimes arises with fishing an island's "point-bars"—for me, anyway—is that they are popular places and can become pretty crowded. Also, there are days when for reasons known only to the fish, all the lights can be on, but nobody's home. Those are times best spent prospecting any non-conformities that might occur in the troughs and bars along the surf line. Just remember that no matter how appealing and inviting any of the bars and submerged points might seem—and no matter how often you have come across reds in such places—most of the fish will be in the deeper water. The bars just tend to keep them there.

The bars found well offshore of the mouths of passes and coastal rivers must be worked from a boat—at least the ones I know of must be. These are surely not as accessible as the surf-side bars and at times cannot be fished safely due to adverse sea conditions. However, a bar out in open water collects bait and predators at least as well as those attached to points of land or in the surf. That is evident by the successes some friends and I enjoyed at a bar that was literally "out in the middle of the ocean"! Actually, it defined the mouth of a large bay, though a lot farther offshore than one might imagine, and it was a summer jewel if there ever was one.

Reds of all sizes can be found on both sides of a bar like that one, and their positioning doesn't seem to be determined by the direction of tidal flow. Finding them requires covering water, and here, that is best done as it is in the interior: by draining your trolling motor's batteries.

If the swells do not cause the trolling motor to cavitate, it is usually best to begin work on the surfside of such a bar. That's usually—usually!—where the biggest of the beasts will be found. Of course, if you notice commotion from mullet or menhaden along its backside—and if there is a place nearby where you can get through or around the bar—then move over there as quickly as you can!

And here, if water clarity and sea conditions permit, you should not ever never in no way resist the howl of the Dog! Indeed, it was at such a place where I have seen several—nay, numerous bulls in the 25- to 30-pound class taken on surface lures! And folks, when it comes to redfish, it *doesn't* get any better than that! Well, not unless those surface lures are fly-rod poppers! On such a bar's backside, work water around 2 feet deep. Any shallower will result in small fish, any deeper might cause some aggravations with big specks. Sure wouldn't want that, would we?

One final note. While beachfront sandbars and their associated troughs—no matter whether they are attached to dry land or are a part of the "sequence"—can be safely waded with a bit of caution, those found near the mouths of passes and rivers and "out in the middle of the ocean" are best worked while in the comfort (spell that s-a-f-e-t-y!) of a boat. Those places can be bull shark city—heed that, too!

Other forms of prime redfish structure can be found near and within these waters. Granted, they will not be found throughout the fish's entire range, but where they are found—mercy!

CHAPTER 8

Jetties

Everyone who has fished for some length of time and managed to catch a few "somethings" assuredly has his or her favorite spots. One of mine—actually just about any that reach a tad bit offshore—is a particular jetty. There are lots of reasons why these long, narrow strips of limestone and granite bounders have attained this pinnacle of preference, but two of them outshine the others: my erstwhile state record fly-caught redfish, and my present state record fly-caught king mackerel. Both weighed 36 pounds even, and both are very deserving of a tale.

The king was the result of an action-packed conventional trip. Since these pages are not intended to expound on the pros and cons of fly fishing for Mr. Teeth, I will declare only that I felt if they were so hell-bent on destroying our conventional lures that day, they should feel exactly the same about some similar-sized and similarly presented flies. It turned out they did, and thank you very much!

My buddy Bubby was with me on that trip as well as the one when I got the big red. Kings had been strangely absent that picture-perfect November day, so we were closely working the jetty's drop-off when the fish bit. When I set the hook, the red made two head shakes that sent vibrations all the way up to the fillings in my teeth, leaving me with no doubts that it was much larger than the 22-pounder I had caught on fly a few days earlier.

Was it ever!

In truth, a lot of luck was involved with the capture of both of those grand fish, though in a way most folks would never consider. The odds of my flies entering their "window" without being preemptively eaten by one of the literally countless creatures—of both species—in the 20- to 30-pound range that are found along that particular jetty during autumn are, at least to me, incomprehensible. So someone (no matter how good) would have to be much luckier than I am to catch a bigger red or king here. Nevertheless, he could easily wear himself slap out wrestling with those "baby beasts," and that's what makes this and others like it such great ones.

The fishery is created by a combination of environment and events. Jetties, no matter if they are found inshore or offshore, are usually created to protect docking areas or to stabilize channels for shipping traffic. They are invariably much "different" from anything else in the neighborhood and are therefore fish attractors of the first order, providing cover for numerous prey species. Jetties that are intended to maintain the depth of the channel through a coastal river's mouth attract freshwater species such as shad and skipjack herring as well as those found in saltwater such as menhaden, mullet, and sardines. Then too, in some areas the striped mullet begin to form their spawning aggregations during autumn, and in their movements hither and yon they regularly come upon the barriers the jetties create, adding their often huge numbers to the predators' menu. Similar events concerning saltwater prey species also occur around jetties extending offshore a ways.

Both bull reds and juveniles can be present virtually year-round along an offshore-reaching jetty, especially in the more temperate areas of our coast. Nevertheless, their numbers and potential size tend to increase markedly during autumn. This is in great part a result of an increase in the number of transient fish that have pursued prey to the confines of the jetty and have remained there.

There are three techniques that are effective here. Upon arriving at a jetty, you will probably notice a gathering of boats near its end or at some other particular and rather localized spot. Their crews are bottom fishing, and that is indeed a fine way to pass a pleasant autumn day—or summer day, for that matter—catching reds. Admittedly it is not my preferred tactic, though I have indulged in it occasionally and have enjoyed myself immensely each time—one, especially.

An old-time fishing buddy was the boss of a local oil field service company. He liked to fish—almost to the point of excess. His crew worked seven days on and seven days off and lived—and ate—at the shop during their seven days on. To "cut costs" occasionally, my buddy would feed them fresh fish.

He rang my phone one afternoon, requesting my presence on such a "meat run." His thoughts that day were on amassing a mess of reds from a favorite jetty—and did I have any bait? Four frozen mullet, I responded. Good enough, he guessed.

We and our four frozen mullet arrived at the point of the jetty at around 3 o'clock that afternoon—and I won't say a word about the feasibility of making a one-way run of almost an hour with such a limited amount of bait aboard! Nevertheless, an hour or so later we were headed home with four big reds in the cooler, two of which were baby bulls. All four of them were taken on the mullets' heads, and guess which crew member was allowed to fish the first three heads before the other crew member wised up to the situation.

So in case you haven't been paying attention to what I've recommended a few times earlier herein as a natural bait for bull

Jetties can provide outstanding action with reds of all sizes.
Several patterns are time-proven.

reds, I'll remind you: *mullet heads*! With, perhaps, an inch of
shoulder attached, but no more than that. Hooked from bottom
to top through both lips, it stays on the hook better than the
body parts that are found aft, and it puts out a pretty good stink.
Fresh mullet heads, though, are usually much better than frozen
ones. Still, you sure don't want to back out of a trip because that's
all you have on hand!

But four, again, is a bit on the skimpy side.

Anyway, when fishing bottom along a jetty, its best to fish
your *mullet heads* on a breakaway rig. Not particularly caring for
three-way swivels, I tie my line to one end of a plain black barrel swivel. Then I tie around 3 feet of 40- or 50-pound fluorocarbon to the other end of the swivel and finish that off with a

size 8/0 circle hook. Finally, I tie about a foot of 12- or 15-pound mono to the "line end" of the swivel and add a 1-ounce or there-abouts swivel sinker to that. If the sinker fouls in the rocks, you can break it off without losing the entire terminal assembly. At least, that how it's supposed to work.

The second way to fish a jetty is to troll large wiggling lures such as CD18 Magnum Rapalas alongside it. During fall it's best to deploy only two, as the potential for a multiple hook-up with both bull reds and king mackerel increases with the number of lures in the water, and two is plenty enough if you fish from a 20-foot bay boat, as I do.

At this time it's usually best to fish these lures on around 5 feet of wire for insurance against bite-offs by kings. Sixty- to 90-pound single-strand is a good choice; affix the lure to one end with a haywire twist and create a tight loop in the other end for attaching to the line with a black ball-bearing snap swivel. Set one lure back for about 10 seconds, the other just far enough so that the swivel is right at the water's surface. That will put the lure right in the wheel wash, and no, it certainly won't pick up many reds—not normally, anyway. But I simply cannot allow all those king mackerel to go unmolested, and it will entice them. If you don't want to be overly entertained by Mr. Teeth (you cannot eliminate him altogether when trolling many offshore jetties during autumn), then set the second wiggler back for some eight seconds, and don't make any tight turns!

With its centerline some 30 feet from the jetty's water line, troll a slim "S" pattern at about 3 knots both up and down the structure. The opposing tracks can cause the lures to be affected somewhat differently by the current, and whatever that difference might be could be just enough to inspire a big brawny bull to bite.

Here, as with Technique #3, you should immediately mark the particular spot where a strike occurs. While a handheld GPS unit will suffice, taking note of features on the jetty is a better method—at least it is for those of us who are, shall we say, a little slow on the draw. Eye-catching objects such as overly large or strange-shaped boulders, particularly high or low spots in the rocks, or an unusual "painting" courtesy of the gulls, terns, and pelicans have been used with fine results. Upon relieving yourself of the originator of the strike in whatever way you so choose, immediately make another pass across "the mark."

Technique #3 is by far my favorite, since I can *fly-fish* while performing it. Hey, do you know how hard it's been to keep from talking about that more often? You should be proud of me. Anyway, here you must have some clue about what you are doing, and that requires an understanding of the general shape of an offshore jetty. So . . .

A cross-section of such a jetty is basically triangular, with the wide base resting on the seabed. The slope of its sides causes it to decrease in width as it nears the waterline and subsequently reaches its apex. Fish can be found at any point along its slope; therefore—since this is a casting exercise—you should not become obsessed with working your lures close to the visible part of the jetty along its waterline.

Rather, while on the trolling motor and moving against any current that is present, position the boat some 30 feet outside the jetty and make your casts to points roughly 6 to 8 feet from it and ahead of you. That allows the lures to be retrieved at an angle across the jetty's slope—*provided* you allow the lure to work progressively deeper as it is being drawn toward the boat.

While you are thus working the jetty's slope—and, for that matter, any other time you are fishing an offshore jetty—you should always be on the lookout for schools of reds on the surface. These fish—bulls and "regular" reds alike—seem to patrol these waters like that and can appear at any time. So can "escorts," that follow a hooked fish to the surface.

Both of these well-appreciated events are usually fairly short-lived, so you must be properly prepared for the opportunity they offer. An encounter with patrolling fish does not usually present any problems—as long as they are detected before they pass just beneath the boat. On the other hand, escorts are often first noted with a landing net rather than a rod in hand.

Never leave your rod in the back of the boat to net a fish that your friend in the front of the boat has hooked! *Always* carry it forward with you and rest it in an easily accessible spot while you are doing the honors. Should an escort appear with the hooked fish, quickly dispose of the net (your companion's fish will probably stay hooked, though said companion may not approve of the move), pick up your rod, and flip your jig into the midst of the following fish. If you are fast enough, you are lifetime guaranteed to hook one.

Then both of you can worry about how you are going to get them into the boat!

While you should always be on the lookout for fish suddenly appearing alongside a jetty, you should also keep an ear peeled for strange noises. Son-in-law and I had been having a particularly rambunctious day, and the action finally subsided. We then began drifting along the rocks, probing the depths alongside the jetty with our jigs, when both of us began hearing something other than the sound of the gentle breaking swells. It was so strange—and continuous—that we decided to try to locate its source. Eventually we discovered a bull red trying rather unsuccessfully to eat a fairly large crab that was swimming on the surface—quite entertaining except, perhaps, for the crab. Anyway, in an attempt to be a good Samaritan, son-in-law pitched his jig at the red, hooked it, and during the procedure of wrestling it to the boat, the crab escaped.

Here's another scenario that I have encountered numerous times around an offshore jetty during autumn, compliments of a high-resolution color depth recorder. Trolling innocently along, occasionally scanning the barren surface and the recorder's blank screen for signs of impending action, you are suddenly shocked to see the bottom half of the recorder's screen turn solid red. Thinking there surely must be a major malfunction therein, you start doodling with it, and roughly two and a half seconds later both trolling rods deck. Party time!

I have no clue how many reds it takes to turn the bottom half of a Si-Tex CVS106's screen solid red, but every time I have witnessed such a phenomenon, a definite change for the better was imminent! To enjoy the most of it, once the fish on the trolling gear have been properly disposed of, relocate the school and work them over with jigs on lighter tackle, staying with them with the aid of the machine. Most fish I have encountered in the big red blobs have been juveniles and "baby bulls," but you can beat yourself to the bone catching them.

Like I said, during fall it's hard to beat a jetty.

So what's their status during summer—the time of vacations and normally the most settled and fishable weather? Would you believe they can be almost as good in summer as they are in the fall? In truth, though, most of my recent summer forays to offshore jetties were bail-outs after discovering the waters farther offshore were a bit too lumpy for my taste. One of those trips resulted from my son-in-law's visit to participate in a saltwater fishing tournament. The second day of the event was drop-dead gorgeous, and while we were running the offshore current lines, he got a cobia that eventually netted him the second-place trophy in that category. Conditions on the third and final day, though, were radically different.

After beating our way a mile or so offshore of the mouth of the pass—and while doing so noticing a boat much larger than mine reverse course after apparently opting for Plan B, we followed suit. An hour or so later, we ducked around the end of our favorite jetty and not unexpectedly found a pocket of calm, clear water.

My log book indicates that by working the slope of the jetty's rocks with $\frac{1}{2}$-ounce jigs on heavy casting tackle, we caught four bull reds in the 20- to 30-pound class, all being released, as none were big enough to enter into the tournament. We also got a 20-pound king, several Spanish macks, ladyfish and hardtails, a 20-inch speck, and a small grouper. Not too shabby for a bail-out trip that began late and ended early so that we could attend the event's final weigh-in!

Bail-outs are one thing; directed efforts are not necessarily another, and jetties do not often discriminate between the two. Friends from the Florida Keys and Houston were once down for an extended offshore fishing session, the weather throughout it was perfect, and a particularly favorite section of nearby ocean was at its best. But around noon on their second day, the guy from Florida said he'd like to catch some redfish. So I relented and headed toward my friendly and reliable jetty where, by bumping shrimp-tipped jigs on the bottom of a hole at the end of the rocks, he and his Texas compadre quickly caught six—all very nice fish, though not quite bulls—before I was able to convince them to quit that easy fishing and renew the quest for the offshore beasties. Incidentally, that was one of the most easily accomplished redfish missions I ever undertook, but again, it was not surprising.

I did end up feeling a little guilty on a trip a while back with a stockbroker/hunting/fishing buddy and his son-in-law. He had asked me to "show the boy around," so since it was such a fine day we headed—guess where—in search of bull reds. And as is usually the case, they were there—proven by my taking a 16-pounder and then a real beauty estimated at around 35 before it was released. Although my companions did have action, sadly it was provided by the lesser types. So that brings us to the point where discussion on how to appease the reds and at the same time avert (somewhat) the "lesser types" that are present here, often in great numbers, during summer is in order.

To begin with, even during summer, jetties standing in relatively deep water are not especially good places to fish if you intend to acquire some skillet material. Indeed, recently it has become quite difficult to catch more than a couple of legal fish from the waters around my favorite jetty on any given trip—most are considerably larger. That fact, plus the very good probability that a few of the other large, tackle-testing types present here will also be entertaining you, makes these places best suited for fun and frolic rather than for fillets.

That being the case, you should arm yourself with tackle that is up to the task. I carry two casting outfits when I am not fly fishing jetties: a $6\frac{1}{2}$-foot, medium-heavy "pitching stick" with a top-line reel holding 200 yards of 17-pound mono and a $6\frac{1}{2}$-foot, extra-heavy muskie rod with a top-line reel one size larger than the other and holding around 175 yards of 30-pound mono.

I prefer my guests use the lighter outfit. Given my age and physical condition, I like to use something with which I can lean on a big fish so I can whip it and send it back home before it whips me! Same goes with fly tackle—12-weight and well appreciated!

Whatever outfit you decide to use, rely on a short length of clear green 50-pound fluorocarbon for a fray-resistant leader. However, if you get a couple of snip-offs from suspected kings, replace the mono leader with a foot or so of 60-pound single-strand wire fashioned in the same manner as recommended for trolling. Jigs in the $\frac{3}{8}$- or $\frac{1}{2}$-ounce range are favored; use the lightest you can cast effectively and that will reach bottom in any current that may be present. Four-inch, minnow-shaped plastic grubs are good choices.

Just in case someone is curious, in some areas there are (or once were) fishing piers built through and a short way beyond the surf. Those in no way resemble jetties, and their life expectancy is considerably shorter—at least, the few I have known have been abruptly terminated at times. Still, they present a form of hard structure and therefore can attract both prey and predators, and occasionally someone actually catches a good one from such a pier. They do provide a place to fish for folks who are limited in their ability to access saltwater areas, so they do serve a purpose.

If this opportunity has some appeal, understand that the walkway of such a pier is elevated well above the water's surface, and that makes fishing for large types like bull reds somewhat difficult because the "angle thing" favors the fish. Besides the fairly heavy gear that is normally required, some sort of landing device is necessary, and I have no intention of delving into those oddball creations. If you do manage to hook a bull, give a little prayer that someone nearby has such a gizmo. Almost invariably, this is a bottom-fishing endeavor utilizing natural baits. Do you remember how to spell "natural baits"? M-U-L-L-E-T H-E-A-D-S!

At present I have no clue where or if any surfside piers still exist. They simply present (ed?) an opportunity that I felt should be included herein. If you are serious about your redfishing and have any other option—any!—avoid them.

While I'm on "manmade things in the surf," I might as well touch on the structures that have been created in some areas to prevent beach erosion. Like jetties, these are usually made of boulders; unlike jetties, they usually parallel the beach. Those that have been around a while normally have built sandy shallows between them and the beach, but the water just offshore is often plenty deep enough to hold reds, among other species. If that is so—and you should be able to determine this by the water's hue—these structures can produce action on both the rising and the falling tide—just as long as some amount of current sweeps the rocks, and they can typically be fished from a boat as well as by wading. Jigs and spoons are normally the best bets for reds. These features are subject to being overrun at times by beach bunnies, so target them when that pestilence is prone to be holed up in their concrete warrens.

III

Reds
for All
Seasons

CHAPTER 9

Spring

In many places where they are found, redfish provide a year-round opportunity, though the productive ways and means can vary radically with the seasons. On the other hand, in some areas you can drag a spoon or a spinnerbait across a jumble of oysters and catch them whenever you feel like fishing. Well, almost—and except, perhaps, during spring.

I chose to begin these chapters on seasonal techniques with spring, the only reason being so that I can get it behind me and move on to more personally appealing times of year. Yes, I have caught a number of reds during past springs—big ones, too. However, most have been taken during "historically recent" springs. In other words, for a period that was longer than I intend to relate, I had fits catching enough reds in the springtime for Sunday dinner, much less for Friday soup. I blame that on one particular factor that took a very long time for me to fully comprehend:

Spring begins one day after winter and ends one day before summer!

In case the relevance of that profound statement temporarily eludes you, I feel that the best explanation will be to divide this chapter in half—"early spring" and "late spring"—because weather-wise, early spring is a world apart from late spring. That difference assuredly affects redfish behavior and how fishing folks can best adjust to it.

So . . .

Early Spring

To begin with, do not expect these lines to contain any references to the temperature's effect on redfish. Reds can tolerate a wide range of temperatures and will feed throughout them when they can—possibly snacking rather than gorging when exposed to both ends of the scale, but still actively eating. Simply put, if it's too cold or too hot for redfish to feed, then it's far too cold or too hot for you to be fishing! Otherwise, since they are creatures of the shallows, that is where they will usually feed. Trouble is, those "shallows" don't stay the same for long.

During the first part of early spring, cold fronts with their corresponding offshore winds create low tides. Those, when combined with the day's "actual" low tide, can completely drain an ideal feeding area. Nearby waters, though, which are normally too deep for the reds' preferences, can become prime target areas at this time, especially where any form of benthic structure is present.

Some of those cold fronts may still be pretty chilly, and because of that my erstwhile erroneous practices focused on the edges of much deeper water—where, notably, redfish were often present in numbers during winter. There will be more on that topic in Chapter 12, but suffice it to say that at the time I presumed that since reds had been holding to such edges during some pretty chilly winter days, they should still be doing the same on comparably cold early spring days. It took a long time for me to discover that they weren't! They had moved to much shallower areas and remained near them during these increasingly brief periods of very low tides.

So, on low-tide days, a worthwhile practice is to work the edges of the "dry flats" and similar feeding grounds with a bow-mounted trolling motor. Cover ground with "quick strike" lures such as spoons and spinnerbaits—long stretches of barren water often lie between schools of fish. A surprisingly effective technique for prospecting the rims of small to medium-sized bays arises at this time. At high idle or a bit more speed, move along the shoreline some 15 to 20 feet from it as the water's depth there allows. When you "blow out" some fish—you'll know it when you do!—immediately shut down the outboard and wait quietly for five or six minutes. Then—again with the trolling motor—make a semicircular sweep well outside of the point where the fish flushed, then slowly and quietly move back toward the bank and continue slowly along in the direction the fish had moved, prospecting all the while with a spoon or spinnerbait. It works—now, and during winter! However, once the water warms up a bit, that procedure will likely as not run 'em into the next bay, so be advised!

Early "early spring" actually gave me far fewer hard times than late "early spring," mainly because of those low tides and the similarity of fishing them then and during winter, which has always been a very successful time for me. Conversely, though, as Aprils waxed, the cold fronts became noticeably less frequent, often much less intense, and between them the tide rose. And it often got pretty damn high!

When it did—and still does—reds can go just about anywhere they want to—for sure, they can get into places where you can't. Not unless you can wade after them! And that is an option, in areas with a firm bottom. The key here is to follow the fish as I described in Chapter 1—follow the rising water into the shallowest areas you can find.

Flooded grass often holds fish, but they will probably be scattered, and the high water can mask indications of their presence. Therefore there is now very little opportunity here for either sight fishing or effective blind-casting. At such times, a more angler-friendly target area is the shorelines of tidal cuts whose banks are solid dirt, sand, or shells, with any adjacent grass being above the high-water mark. These banks serve to block and confine prey that reds have herded against them. They are usually best when there is tidal movement through the cut, and any indication of minnows swim-

During early spring, cold weather can lead to hot action with reds.

ming erratically along the surface near the banks justifies some speculative casts, which are usually best when made parallel to and near the shoreline. Don't expect to find fish in gangs here, but it's a pattern that can produce some action during otherwise hard times—just like a few speculative casts around your favorite junk pile! Those little sweet spots can be the best of trip savers throughout spring.

Likewise, early spring is a great time for making a trip to your friendly local barrier island. Now, both the surf and any backside marshes that may be present there can hold reds in very worthwhile numbers. Also, the little nasties that become such a nuisance—or such a concern—along the seashore once the water warms up a bit are relatively scarce now. Just keep a weather eye out to prevent getting caught in one of the seasonal unpleasantries that take place anywhere along the coast.

On that note, I must describe a trip some friends made to a favorite island—a trip, incidentally, on which I was invited but very regretfully had to pass. The weather forecast was iffy, but the fishing had been hot, so they sortied in a 26-foot, deep-vee center console rig powered by twin outboards—a highly recommended mode of transportation for this scenario. They arrived at the island just in time to meet a screaming norther head-on, moved the boat to safe anchorage in a pocket within the island, and then, not surprisingly, the tide went out—a *long* way out! The boat subsequently grounded, the fishing immediately went to hell in a handbasket, and with only water and snack crackers aboard, it was a long and awfully boring 24 hours before the tide came up enough to refloat the boat and let them escape.

On a trip to a barrier island at this time—which, at least for me, is awfully hard to resist—you may get caught in such a situation, but you can make the best of it by carrying along some emergency provisions—sandwiches, complete raingear, plenty of water, and a cell phone to alert those who need to know of your plight. Then just wait it out! Don't try anything foolish—like a run back home in the teeth of the gale—that can get you into more trouble than you are already in. It will abate—be patient.

Fortunately—at least for those folks who are not of the mindset to catch redfish or nothing at all, the high-tide periods of late early spring offer a fine opportunity for specks. And pursuing them—usually around oysters or while they are running shrimp on the surface, and almost exclusively with either surface lures or flies—is how I often spend April days with tolerable weather. Besides the potential for the year's biggest speck being excellent now, there is usually plenty of prime skillet material available. And I do like to eat 'em!

Anyway, late spring eventually arrives and with it some

slightly better weather and some very different ways and means to catch reds.

Late Spring

One of the most notable changes between, say, mid-May and mid-April is seen in the effectiveness of surface lures, which become more consistently productive now. "Consistently" is the key word here, since topwaters are effective throughout the year, even during winter—at times! Now, with weather and water conditions becoming more favorable for their use, they become a primary source of entertainment, around the shallow perimeters of bays, in the marsh, and even in the up-country!

While reds can be found in up-country waters during early spring, the season's rapidly fluctuating tides prevent the fish from becoming established there—here today, gone tomorrow, so to speak. In late spring, though, with the flats-draining northers becoming much less frequent, this area begins to gather and hold more and more reds. Indeed, the up-country presents a fine option for those defeating super-high-tide days that can still occur now, though much less often. Here, even in the high water, clarity is often good enough for sight-fishing, and the submergent grasses that can blanket much of these areas by midsummer have yet to become much of a deterrent, allowing Top Dogs and such to run unfettered. Then too, the warming temperature and stabilizing depth of the water here brings on a profusion of prey, and the reds eat well. But on that note, if only partial interest is being shown to your Dog, scale down to a "pup"—something considerably smaller than you would normally use. The reds can become keyed on small prey now—not often, but sometimes, so be aware.

And be prepared!

On that note, I must declare that late spring—say, beginning between early and mid-May—is a grand time to fly fish for reds in the interior. The weather and water conditions are growing more frequently favorable for doing so, and the fish seem more disposed to showing some bootie and therefore creating excellent sight-fishing opportunities. Also, using smaller flies to match the smaller bait makes accurate presentation to the fish easier and the fly's entry less likely to spook them. This is the time when, during my younger and less educated days, things began to quickly turn from rags to riches, especially when I chose to fly fish!

As late spring begins to favor summer, sight-fishing along the edges of interior bays, in marshes, and in up-country waters gets as hot as the weather. The action is often dependent on tidal movement—frequently the falling stage, but it can be quite good in early morning, no matter what the tide is doing. This is a great time for sight-fishing, because any prevailing breezes tend to be light or nonexistent now and fishy indications are relatively easy to spot. Once any tailing or other signs of feeding fish cease, try blind-casting along the edges of matted submergent grass or around accumulations of oysters, both in no more than 2 feet of water. Lightweight spinnerbaits or buzzbaits are usually appropriate in both the sight-fishing and the blind-casting settings.

While the action increases notably in the marsh and up-country during late spring, my experiences have shown that it tapers off considerably in the area around the seashore, both in the surf and in backside waters. Don't know why, since I've taken some pretty beefy bulls and plenty of "regular" reds alongside jetties in May, and many of those structures extend through the surf. Whatever, with that exception—and possibly also the waters around passes when the weather permits fishing them, most action with regular reds, at least, will take place inshore. The seashore gets much better during summer.

Still, most folks fish for reds most often in inshore waters, and even in late spring, abnormally high tides therein can make for some tough times. Maybe my dearth of spring action so long ago was caused simply by my fishing for the red rascals any time

I could and not caring a whit what the tide was doing at the time. For sure, throughout my life, one of my most steadfast philosophies on the matter has been to fish when I could, not just when some favorable weather pattern arose. Of course, if those two particulars happened to coincide, that was just fine with me! Anyway, I caught a lot of fish that way.

So for these purposes I feel I should amend that philosophy a bit. "Throughout spring, fish when you can, and if the tide happens to be low, then give thanks and give the reds hell. If it isn't, then forget about the reds and give the specks hell!"

And that's more than enough on spring.

CHAPTER 10

Red-Hot Times

My old fly-fishing buddy Capt. Bubby Rodriguez and I had spent the entire morning running around some close-in offshore grounds in my bay boat, looking for anything—anything!—that might harbor a tripletail or a cobia. Apparently it was one of those "litter-free" days you occasionally encounter if you do that kind of stuff often enough, so about the time the tide should have begun falling, I suggested we stow the big sticks, break out the lighter gear, and head inshore to try one of my little sweet spots for some specks.

By the time we reached it, conditions were near perfect with a fairly strong current sweeping along various small prey species, bright sunshine, and glassy water—and it was hotter than Celine Dion. However, the fishing there was as cold as the proverbial polar bear's butt. Strike two!

Back then, ol' Bubby guided fly-fishing trips for redfish for a living. On his days off (or when he rebooked a trip so he could go offshore with me!) he liked to do "something different"—like run around the ocean all morning looking for floating junk and something beneath it to throw a fly at. So I was hesitant to offer him my third pitch: a narrow, shallow, meandering tidal cut where I had found a gang of nice reds on a couple of trips in similar conditions earlier that summer. But it was either that or head home, and since neither of us was quite ready to do that, he suggested we give it a try.

Once again the high, falling tide had drawn the water in the adjacent marsh into the cut, making it much clearer than the open-water areas nearby. In it, reds could be easily seen more than 50 feet away, and sight-fishing for them was excellent. Bubby said the setting made it different enough to make his day. Me? I had a ball, just watching, as several of the fish ate him slap up. Great spectator sport!

Every year, it seems that high summer brings temperatures that average a bit warmer than those of the previous year. Global warming or not, and taking into account a redfish's ability to tolerate some pretty extreme weather, by midsummer the water in many coastal areas is so high in temperature and so low in dissolved oxygen that even the reds are becoming rather uncomfortable. Knowing where and when that state of discomfort is at its lowest level will lead to the best action to be had with them. The tidal cut mentioned earlier is a good starting point.

As it was being pulled into the cut, the water in the grass—which was partially shaded—*could* have been a bit cooler than the water it was displacing. That *could* have lowered the temperature in the cut just enough to trigger a bite—or it may not have made an iota of difference, and the fish bit because they could easily detect the flies as the water cleared. One thing that is likely, though, is that the water being drawn into the cut from the marsh had more dissolved oxygen in it than the water that was in the cut before the tide began to fall.

Relatively narrow, shallow tidal cuts like that one have been the salvation of many summer trips for me over the years. One reason for that is I frequently make those trips to fish with flies, and in my part of the world, fly fishing in the marsh is best done on the falling tide. Incidentally, during summer hereabouts that normally takes place in the afternoon—the hottest time of the day!

There is a world of difference in the productivity as well as the character of smallish, fairly shallow, and meandering tidal cuts between high and low tides. Therefore I must advise that if you try one of them before the water has fallen a good bit and—if it normally suffers from turbidity during higher stages—before it has cleared somewhat (roughly the first half of the falling period will usually create those conditions), don't be surprised if all you accomplish is a waste of good time. On the other hand, in many areas of the marsh the water adjacent to such cuts supports lush growths of various submergent grasses. These act as filters, and the water remains reasonably clear during all stages of the tide, both in the marsh and in the cuts. The water is also fairly well oxygenated, even though its temperature can get pretty warm! Here, good action is possible throughout the entire falling tide.

The area of marsh where Bubby takes his clients is like that. Redfish inhabit it at all times, except when winter northers have drained it, but just because they inhabit it does not mean they can be caught there with ease.

While most often during summer Bubby comes south to fish with me on his "days off," occasionally I will make a trip north to fish with him. We leave the launch site at reasonable daylight and usually have caught a fish or two by sunrise.

It is quite pleasant in the marsh at that time. Typically it is the coolest part of the day, and it is frequently slick calm and therefore easy to see working fish—and there have been occasions when we could see tails just about everywhere we looked until around 8 o'clock. During that time—if our casting was decent and if we didn't make too many long-distance releases— we have taken as many as a dozen nice reds. But between 8 and 10 o'clock we typically see fewer and fewer working fish, and after that they lay up, burying themselves in the submerged grass to wait out the hottest part of the day.

I've watched them do exactly that during summer in numerous other, rather fresh interior marshes for decades. As with "Bubby's marsh," the tide has little apparent effect on clarity, temperature, or dissolved oxygen, so when it begins to get hot, the fish turn off. That means you should fish areas like this very early in the morning for best results, and that was the way I had normally fished during this time. However, an incident with Bubby and another friend once illustrated that with patience, precision, and stealth you can catch reds when they are "laid up" in the heat of the day.

It was getting on toward noon—bright, hot, humid, and without a hint of a breeze—and after the early morning's festivities had ended, pickings became pretty slim. Then Bubby—who was on the poling platform—went on point, gently spudded down the pole, and softly said "There's a redfish at nine o'clock about twenty feet away." Sure enough, there it was: only a 20-incher or so but plainly visible—once we had located it—partially buried in the widgeon grass.

I wish I could say I caught it, but it was not my turn. Our friend's first cast was about 2 feet in front of the fish, which never acknowledged the fly's presence. Several more casts were surely good enough to be taken by an aggressive fish, but this one appeared to be almost comatose—certainly not aggressive! Finally a cast was made so that the fly was drawn just past the fish's nose. Suddenly it stiffened, flared its gills, and sucked in the fly. Yeah, that was a lot of work for one rather smallish redfish, but it was sure exciting, and it proved they can be caught when they are hunkered down in the salad waiting out the heat.

So did another tactic that I was introduced to a couple of years ago. This was a conventional-fishing exercise and involved stout spinning gear, curly-tail grubs rigged weedless, and an 8-foot stepladder.

Initially, four of us were having some difficulty sight-fishing in a large, grassed-up pond due to both some thick overcast and the reluctance of the fish to cooperate. A big squall soon sent us scurrying back to the marina—where, while we were waiting out the storm, our host fetched the ladder. We soon returned to our pond, where he then secured the ladder on the bow's casting platform, ascended it, perched atop it like a pelican on a piling, and thus began the search. Due to his elevated observation point, he had some great sight-fishing action throughout the rest of the day. Down below, we continued to have next to none unless our guy in the crow's nest pointed out a fish for us. The difference in subsurface visibility was, not altogether surprisingly, amazing!

Now I certainly cannot advocate the use of an 8-foot stepladder in a bay boat for the purpose of sight-fishing for reds, no matter how well it works. Assuredly, if I did some klutz would try it, fall off and get a boo-boo, and sue everyone old enough to own a wallet. However, just in case you carry an 8-foot stepladder on board your bay-boat . . .

Here's another tactic that might be worthwhile for those of you who don't fish with flies. (I learned right on that fly fishing doesn't work too well from atop a ladder!)

This one involved nicely visible fish, none of which would respond to lures—not even Tiny Torpedoes and spinnerbaits, surprisingly enough—being retrieved closely enough to them to gain their interest except to be spooked by them.

The solution was a spinning outfit, a size 1 hook tied directly to the 12-pound line, and a fresh shrimp of roughly 50- or 60-count threaded onto the hook. This was lobbed just past and ahead of a redfish, drawn toward it, and then allowed to soak right in front of the fish's nose. Yes, the line became so twisted from the swivel-less rig that I had to replace it for the next trip, but the technique got the attention of enough redfish to justify it.

Fish in grass-choked interior waters may feed again briefly at dusk during summer, but by that time I, at least, have usually eaten supper and am well into a decent cigar. However, summer is the time for afternoon squalls, and it is not uncommon for the sky to

An approaching squall After the squall has passed
is a great time to fish for reds, because the rain will have
cooled and oxygenated the water.

remain thickly overcast after the rain and neon display has ended. If you have the capability to make a trip at this time, you may encounter fishing that is as explosive as it is in the early morning.

Of course, with the overcast sky there won't be any sight-fishing unless the reds are considerate enough to show you a little bootie. This is usually strictly blind-casting, and if you have ready access to an area with a lot of submerged vegetation, shame on you if you fish it with anything but a buzzbait!

The "post-squall opportunity" is created by the combination of the water being slightly cooled and oxygenated by the rainfall and the fact that the sun—which is shielded by the overcast—isn't heating it right back up again. I was fortunate to live in a place where I was able to take advantage of this scenario many times, and I have *never*—spell that n-e-v-e-r—missed when I did! Reds may be bulletproof, but they do seem to appreciate the creature comforts.

Sad to say, there will be days when the tide will be wrong, you will assuredly have some honey-dos to take care of in the morning, and if you are going to fish at all, then you must do so in the bright, hot afternoon. In that case, I'd head to the seashore!

One last note. If you aren't all that fond of sweating—or of getting up early to fish the daybreak bite—and if you live reasonably close to a marina or boat basin that has lighted piers, you might seek permission from the harbormaster to try those piers after dark. You are likely to find more specks than reds, and if pilings define the boat slips as well as support the piers, you will lose a good percentage of the larger reds you do hook to shredded lines, but it is another opportunity. Personally, when I decide to try it I use a freshwater "flipping stick," straight 30-pound mono, and set the reel's drag on "stop" instead of "slow." Need I say that hooking a 6-pounder on a 10-foot flip is nothing short of a riot?

But it's only one way to catch reds during summer. Wear a hat, don't forget the sunscreen—at least SPF-30, if you please, drink plenty of water, and have a great time any way you choose.

The reds will help you see to that!

CHAPTER 11

The Autumn Extravaganza

Melee in the Marsh

Autumn is the favorite time of the year for most folks who pursue redfish. Assuredly, one of the reasons for that is the nice weather that can occur between the gradually increasing number and intensity of "cool" fronts. As I have aged a bit, I also find more enjoyment in such creature comforts, but rest assured that there's more to autumn favoritism than the pleasures of crisp temperatures, unblemished skies, and delightfully clear water. The redfish tend to go nuts, then.

I guess if I was a red, I would too. The water's temperature is dropping to a more comfortable level—that assuredly makes 'em more frisky. Also, all sorts of tummy-pleasing goodies are becoming more available to the fish on what seems to be a daily basis—there is plenty for them to eat, and it isn't all that hard for them to acquire. Autumn is truly party time for inshore redfish—and it surely ought to be for the inshore redfish anglers.

Autumn can be one of the best times of year for redfishing.

There are several time-proven patterns that arise during autumn, one of which involves the seashore and the biggest of the beasts—and in a few areas some weather that is quite different than that which is anticipated and enjoyed so much in other places. All that will be covered in Part IV, since its particulars are much different from those pertaining to the inshore opportunities that these fish now provide.

Now, with the decreasing amount of plankton and algae in the water and the resultant increasing clarity, sight-fishing can become outstanding. Combine that with the low tides caused by the offshore winds of the passing cool fronts—which present the fish with far fewer places where they can hide from you—and you have a situation that you will dream of throughout the upcoming winter, spring, and summer. It really can be that good!

The productive techniques—blind-casting as well as sight-fishing—are basically similar to those practiced during the rest of the year. Sight-fishing is usually best on the low tides in the ponds—if you can still access them then—and along the edges of the creeks and small "inside" bays. As for the up-country, though, in many areas those waters are rapidly becoming only a source of conversation and speculation for next summer's trips—and, perhaps, duck hunting. So since I have referred to the sight-fishing procedure a time or two already, I'll expound a bit on it now.

First of all, you *do not* have to fish with flies in order to thoroughly enjoy this very entertaining exercise. However, you should follow the same general procedures—and understand that you will be confronted with the same challenges and dilemmas.

Atop the mud bottoms that are typical of much of the interior areas of coastal estuaries, reds are not as easily detectable as they are against bottoms that are made up of sand and, in some cases, shells. Therefore, bright sunlight in combination with the low tide enhances subsurface visibility—which, of course, is necessary to locate a fish if it isn't waving its tail at you or swimming along in the super-shallows with its back exposed. Also, a calm surface helps greatly. All three of these conditions come together

During autumn redfish often feed with abandon and become susceptible to a wide variety of lures and techniques.

along generally south-facing shorelines at midday after the most recent norther has lost most of its punch. The shoreline grass will create a strip of flat water just downwind of it, the sun is brightest at midday, and the tide will be low from the effects of the previously persistent offshore winds. If you have a penchant for casting to fish that you are looking at—as I do—then if at all possible, time your trip to coincide with the convergence of those three conditions. Then, once you reach the area you intend to prospect, take your time doing so. Look around—*all* around—and *be quiet!*

Here, spinnerbaits no heavier than $^3/_{16}$-ounce, feathered Pet 13 Spoons, and the small surface lures mentioned previously are best, though with the surface lures you must not make too much racket or you will spook 'em into the next ocean. A moderately paced retrieve consisting of steady, light twitches usually works well—just make sure the lure is not "attacking" the fish (moving directly toward it). Reds aren't accustomed to having small mullet, killifish, and the like do things like that, and it unsettles 'em a bit!

Blind-cast coverage of the edges of the outer bays, along any grass islands therein, and atop shallow oyster accumulations is a worthwhile option when the tide is too low to ascend much of the marsh. Again, spinnerbaits, surface lures (the larger types, though, like the Dog or full-size Spit'n Image), and popping rigs are good choices here, and believe me, they can generate all the action you can stand!

While sight-fishing is assuredly the most exciting way to catch reds anywhere and anytime you find them, blind-casting will usually account for more fish—usually! It can actually become a no-brainer at times. The key to it all is to focus on areas that are established structure for redfish and to keep the lure in the strike zone for as long as possible.

In many cases, the strike zone is in no more than 3 feet of water along or atop the aforementioned types of structure and most definitely around all forms of oyster accumulations. With grass shorelines and islands, that means you must work your lures roughly parallel to their edges. That makes it a little tough for the guy in the back of the boat, but it works just fine for the guy on the trolling motor.

Once the "aft-man" has had enough of watching his buddy on the bow catching all the reds, he can either elbow his way forward to the point where he can fish in undisturbed water, too, or suggest (as forcefully as the situation warrants) that they go work some nearby oysters. There, they can both concentrate their efforts on the normally most productive depth of around 2 feet. And there's my contribution to the guy in the back of the boat who, once in position to work the oysters, would be well advised to do his prospecting with a Top Dog or Super Spook.

The seasonally clear water, especially of that depth, also allows you to see exactly where the larger clusters of shells lie. As insinuated earlier, there are places within a reef or bed that offer the best cover for any prey species around, and they typically appear as large dark spots within the lighter-hued surrounding area. That does not imply reds will not be found elsewhere, so fan-cast the entire vicinity where the shells are present—just don't ignore those large, dark splotches!

During fall, reds can make sudden appearances in unlikely places. I have taken them early in the season well up in up-country waters—some of those occasions were really mind-boggling, though I got used to it after a few years. Again, though, those delightful events are usually short-lived and become rarer by the day. Still, if you happen to be driving along a road through such places and come across some disturbances on the surface of a nearby creek or canal that seem a bit too large for the creatures that inhabit it, you should immediately find a parking place and prospect the source with a surface lure or spinnerbait. And should you frequently drive along such routes during autumn, that's a really good reason to carry a casting rod with you at all times!

I was enlightened to that lesson the hard way, having to race home to fetch one of mine after I first came across such a ruckus. But after returning to it I caught five beauties—while standing on the shoulder of the road and dodging traffic that occasionally got awfully close to me while interested parties were trying to see just what I was doing. Man, there were some reds in that ditch that afternoon! The reason was apparently a profusion of killifish that the reds had managed to locate and corral in the confines of the roadside canal. That happened a few times since then, too—but only in autumn. Got that?

More often, though, such a melee will occur in the open marsh—rather, near, around, and within sparse patches of emergent grass in large ponds and small bays. I'm not sure about the reason for those, since there isn't much of a "backstop" for the reds to hem the prey against, but I've come across them—very happily, I assure you—in numerous places and almost frequently

A bull redfish melee like this one is sure to get
your adrenaline pumping.

enough. Keep a watchful eye out for them—a pocket-sized pair of 8X 30 or thereabouts field glasses are a worthwhile investment.

During autumn, the marsh—and for a while even the up-country—can provide some of the best action with reds imaginable. That is, until you have fished a coastal river for them then. Those can be on an entirely different level. Higher, reader—*much* higher!

Rolling on the River

Throughout the redfish's inshore range, it's quite possible that the habitat that is most neglected by anglers who pursue them is riverine. While rivers can offer year-round action in some locations, in many cases it's a seasonal thing, with that season almost invariably being late summer into autumn—or thereabouts. During that time, reds—and a few other popular creatures that I have referred to herein from time to time—provide an opportunity that can be outstanding. Here's how it comes about.

With the season's decreasing amount of runoff entering a coastal river from its upstream tributaries, its current slows. Since fresh water lacks sufficient viscosity to suspend sediments, it relies on the speed of its current to transport them. When that becomes too slow to accomplish the task, any sediments that have entered the river fall out of suspension to bottom, and the water becomes clear—at times quite clear.

The reduced current also allows salt water to move upstream along the bottom of the river's distributaries or "passes," eventually intermixing throughout the water column by way of eddies and upwellings. This occasionally affects the river's overall salinity well upstream.

In the river's coastal delta—and perhaps a bit above that—a variety of saltwater species typically follow this intrusion upstream to join the river's residents and create merry mayhem among its prey types. That's where you come in. And while there may be some omissions or additions within that brief estimate of the situation that a hydrologist might not approve of, it's close enough for our purposes herein.

Redfish, which can now be found in these waters in huge numbers, can be handily taken in three ways. The first is deep-jigging in any cuts, creeks, or secondary passes leading off the primary passes. That tactic will be discussed later and in some detail.

The second is to drift or power-drift (trolling-motor-assisted) with the current while working a pass's shoreline drop-offs with spoons like Sprites or crankbaits like Rat-L-Traps and Rattlin' Rapalas. Reds often cruise this feature, making forays after prey that has been flushed and is fleeing to the adjacent shallows or for some unwise reason has left them and entered the nearby deep water. The drop-off is easily determined in most of the passes and lies where the lighter-hued water atop the shoreline shallows suddenly turns deep green. Most strikes should come close to the drop-off, so work it accordingly.

The third technique—my favorite, though far from being the most productive—is again to drift or power-drift with the current just outside the drop-offs, but spot-casting at visible fish that are cruising atop the shoreline "flats." Reds can show up quite plainly against the sandy bottoms that are often present along the passes. While spoons and spinnerbaits are effective in this setting, small surface lures such as Tiny Torpedoes, Skipjacks, and Spit'n Image Jr.'s (and size 1 fly-rod poppers about $2\frac{1}{2}$ inches long!) are hard to beat, both in productivity and in the fun-and-games department. On cloudy days when sight-fishing is difficult, don't be hesitant to work them "blindly" around any docking areas, stumps, or green timber that may be present, just as you would in a lake for bass. If you like using topwaters for those fish in that setting (who doesn't?), then I'll guarantee you will love using them for redfish in this one!

One thing, though. In the deltas of coastal rivers, reds can exhibit some significantly different behavior patterns—even different from being there in the first place. It's not at all unusual for a gang of them to intercept a passing school of shad, among others—on the surface—in mid-channel—just as a school of striped bass or crevalle jacks might do. Keep alert for the white water and shrieking gulls that announce this indication of another true no-brainer while you are working the shorelines of a pass, and don't worry about having to quickly change lures to something more "appropriate" for the occasion. What you are presently speculating with will probably work just fine!

And don't be in a rush to leave the area once the mayhem on the surface appears to be over. A random cast or two across the now quieting water and allowing the lure to sink a little deeper just might pick up a straggler looking for some leftovers. It sure has for me.

Now it's time for a little lesson in deep-jigging in current—a tactic that is frequently unpracticed and almost as frequently totally unknown to many coastal anglers. But it can be the single most effective technique for fishing in coastal river deltas during autumn.

The reason for this technique—and the problems that are an integral part of it—is because the fish usually hold very close to bottom in these waters in an attempt to avoid the main thrust of the current. Most often they will rise only a short distance into the heaviest flow to strike a lure. Getting that lure down to them—and keeping it there without the current above them and the retrieve lifting it out of the strike zone—is the critical factor.

First, however, you must find some fish. That is best accomplished with a depth recorder, though its purpose is more for locating the proper structure than for pinpointing the fish themselves. Look for slight depressions in the bottom along relatively straight stretches of the channel, and for holes downstream of channel-stabilizing weirs and along the outside edge of the channel where it makes a turn. The change in depth does not need to be great—just enough to provide the fish some shelter from the current. Here, most of the fish will usually be found below the upstream edge of such a hole, so set your anchor just above the hole and allow your boat to drift back some 30 to 40 feet—a short cast—downcurrent of that upstream edge.

Those are good spots for prospecting, but the one which is my favorite is where bottom rapidly shelves upward at least 5 feet—more is much better—and then flattens out at a shallower depth. This causes the current to upwell at the point where the shelving begins and therefore creates an area of slow water along bottom from the lip of the "flat" downstream for some distance. Here, I try to set the anchor as close to the lip as possible and again let the boat drift about 40 feet back before tying it off.

In this drill, the boat's positioning is very important, since it permits you to cover the anticipated strike zone by casting as close to directly upcurrent as possible. That allows the lure— normally, but not always, a single jig—to sink quicker and deeper than it could on cross-current or downcurrent casts, since with those the current's drag on the line will slow the jig's descent and cause it to ascend as it is being retrieved. So make your casts upstream, pause to the point where you first feel the jig tag bottom (it may take a few casts to determine this), and retrieve it with short pumps, just fast enough to maintain contact with it. Once the current carries the jig past the boat and it begins to rise, retrieve it quickly for another cast.

That is the regular way of deep-jigging in current and the one that should be practiced steadfastly. However, no rules or techniques in fishing are set in stone. I learned that one day from a friend who, fishing from the back of my boat, could perform the established drill only with some difficulty. So he speculated a technique that I refer to as "the downstream jig." It shouldn't work, but in clear water less than 15 feet or so deep it occasionally does. And I must say it, since these fish can also be prolific in these waters in autumn, it also works quite well for specks. Perhaps after watching the jig above them for some time, suspended and dancing up and down rather tantalizingly, they become aggravated enough with it to sortie into the current to grab it.

Or maybe they don't, and we've just blundered across some very active fish. Whatever, it has worked in the past often enough, so here's the deal. Make your cast directly cross-current, and while the jig is sinking and being swept along by the flow, give it intermittent short pumps. Then, once it has finished its swing in the current and reached a point behind the boat, jig it slowly with short but brisk hops. Do not retrieve any line while doing so, and don't get in a hurry to bring it in for another cast; very often a strike will come after you have been yo-yoing it out there—well off bottom—for some time. As I said, this is not a normal procedure, and it won't work in dingy water. But if for some reason strikes come slowly with the "regular way," give it a try.

Either method, though, requires good "feel," so this is not the place for wimpy rods and heavy (thick) line. Relatively short, fast-action rods made of high-modulus graphite—like the worm rods used in freshwater bass fishing—are made to order for deep-jigging in current. My favorite for years was a $5\frac{1}{2}$-foot Berkley Series One medium-heavy, straight-grip casting rod. With its reel loaded with Spiderwire Fusion—14-pound with the diameter of 10-pound mono—you could almost feel a fish breathe on the jig! The rod was very sensitive; the line had almost no stretch, and its thin diameter offered little area for the current to act upon. That line, however, was subject to fraying, so I used a foot or so of 20-pound fluorocarbon between it and the jig. A triple surgeon's (overhand) knot proved to be a reliable connection between the line and the leader. On that note, I believe that this particular line is no longer offered. If you can't find any, use a "superbraid" in 30/8.

Consideration for the tackle best suited for this fishing even includes the jig. I prefer the round-head type with a short-shank, heavy-wire hook, which is less prone to bending by reds than the longer-shank versions. Dress it with a soft plastic tail of the type and color favored in your particular area.

The weight of the jig-head, though, is probably the most important factor. Always use the lightest that will sink to bottom in the current, since the lighter jig will dance around a little more enticingly than one only a size heavier. And on that note, the rising tide permits the use of the lightest jigs, since it slows the river's current somewhat in downstream deltaic areas. Remember that, and take advantage of it when you can!

As a general rule, in depths to 15 feet or so and in all current scenarios save that caused by a strong falling tide, I'll begin with a $\frac{3}{8}$-ounce jig-head. If that won't get down, I'll go to a $\frac{1}{2}$-ounce one, and if that still isn't enough, some radical alterations in terminal gear are necessary.

Double-Jig Rig

To create a quick and effective double-jig rig, first tie a short Bimini twist in your line. Then take about 3 feet of 20-pound fluorocarbon, double it so that one leg is 6 to 8 inches longer than the other, and with the doubled end tie a double surgeon's loop. Loop this to the Bimini twist, then tie the jig-heads onto the legs with Palomar knots, remembering to add weight by increasing the size of the jig-head on the longer leg only. The other way seems to lead to tangles.

There are two ways to go about it. One is to create a fish-finder rig of sorts. Begin this with a $\frac{1}{2}$-ounce egg-sinker on the line which, if it is a super-braid, should be tied to the swivel with a Palomar knot. Then tie about $1\frac{1}{2}$ feet of 20-pound fluorocarbon to the other end of the swivel and finish it off with a $\frac{1}{4}$-ounce jig/soft plastic combo. However, here—if you happen to be a member of the Cult of Minnowsoakers—you can pin a minnie through the lips on the jig-head. If all that that isn't heavy enough to reach and hold bottom, increase the size of the egg sinker, not the jig-head.

The second way is to create a

"double-jig rig" (see side-bar). This is usually my preference over the fish-finder because it provides better feel, but it is somewhat prone to self-destruct when you hook a good-sized red on each jig! Two $\frac{1}{4}$-ounce or $\frac{3}{8}$-ounce jig-heads are the norm; if any more weight is needed, increase the size of the trailing jig only.

Recalling past successes from the back of my boat—including one when my companion who was in that position really put it on me—the double-rig was being utilized there. Apparently two jigs hopping and dancing about close together above a red or big speck (or a flounder!) are more than they can

The weather and water of late autumn may seem cool to you, but it sure makes the reds bite!

tolerate, current or not. In any case, deep-jigging in the distributaries of coastal rivers now is a proven technique—for anglers in the know! Now you are one of them. See how easy it is?

CHAPTER 12

A Cure for Cabin Fever

Have you ever had "that feeling"—the nagging sensation that you should be somewhere else doing something different? I got it one winter day a while back, and having had it lead me in the right direction a number of times in the past, I yielded, moving the boat from the oyster bed I'd been working to a nearby long, much shallower point and replacing my jig with a Top Dog. And a short time later my efforts were rewarded with the explosive strike and surging fight of a 28-inch redfish. Not a bad way of starting a new year, huh?

Yes, sir! That took place on January 16—a day after two weeks of rapid-fire cold fronts and a day when insulated coveralls were still quite comfortable, thank you very much. Yet that red—along with four others—was caught in less than 2 feet of water and on a very abbreviated trip. Incidentally, all evidence points to "that feeling" being a semiconscious manifestation of past experiences, so get yourself some of these experiences and maybe it will start nagging you!

Throughout much of the winter, many of the marinas along the parts of the coast where fishing remains feasible can at times resemble well-stocked, used-car-and-boat-trailer dealerships. As a result, the popular spots—which are almost invariably deep holes in the local canals, rivers, creeks, and bayous—will often give up a lot of reds, but a lot more *could* be caught by fishing in much shallower water even now, in all but the coldest weather.

Fact is, a redfish's ability to go about his business in some pretty chilly temperatures occasionally gets him caught in areas where he cannot escape quickly enough to some slightly warmer depths. Then he is subject to going into traumatic shock—and often subsequently dies—from the passage of a really cold blast. But then, too, I've caught reds on popping rigs with the jig suspended only some 3 feet when there was skim ice in the shoreline shallows. Reds may not really be bulletproof, but they are a lot tougher than I am!

All that was nicely illustrated on the first day that the air temperature hit 60 degrees after the infamous Christmas Freeze of 1989—roughly a day after more than 70 straight hours of subfreezing temperatures at my old home deep in the Mississippi River Delta. That afternoon I scouted some nearby bays—just to see what the damage had been, and although I did come across a saddening number of dead fish, I also saw plenty that were very much alive. All of them were in water less than 3 feet deep! As I said, reds are tough!

Unfortunately, though, many anglers have become conditioned through the assertions of local media and the misinformation they have read for years in more wide-reaching magazines that the only way to catch these fish during winter is to work the deep holes. Far from it! Assuredly, over the decades I have taken my share of winter reds from a particular deepwater spot that is a winter honey hole without equal in the region. On breezy, chilly days when I am compelled to fish, I still seek shelter along its protected shorelines and slow-pump a deep jig.

But you can safely bet your last Dog that on any reasonably friendly winter day you will find me far from deepwater working oyster beds, and other forms of benthic structure in depths of 5 feet or less—often considerably less, and with flies and frequently with surface lures!

And that's been taking place long before people even knew how to spell "global warming" and well before a recent string of rather temperate winters!

So what's the deal? Why have I been having fine winter action while fishing shallow (as have a few in-the-know guides I am aware of) when the radio, TV, and newspaper gurus continue to tell their audiences to fish deep? Probably because those guys have never broken from tradition. Or if they did, they probably tried the shallows at the wrong time and never caught diddley squat. And when to fish shallow is even more important than where to fish shallow.

"When" is on a reasonably friendly day. Those seldom come during prolonged progressions of short-term cold fronts, and they never come within the duration of a visit from the "Arctic Express." But they certainly can and do occur a couple of days or so after one has blown itself out, and in relatively southern latitudes along our coast, periods of a week or more of very fishable weather are not unheard of. Just remember that on the chilly days, bright sunlight is a major factor for decent fishing, and the brightest period—which radiationally warms the water, causing the fish to become more active—occurs roughly between 10 AM and 1 PM. On some pretty chilly days, foot-deep flats may not surprisingly be devoid of redfish before 10 o'clock, offer excellent sight-fishing for them between then and 1 o'clock, and progressively become less productive afterwards as the sun dips and begins to lose its warming effects.

The rising tide is another major factor in when to fish shallow. A promising accumulation of oysters, a sunken boat, derelict oil field rubble where that is found, or the submerged remains of

Redfish can be quite cooperative on warmer winter days.
The key is to fish lures slowly.

a dilapidated fishing camp—all prime winter redfish structure—
might seem barren on low, slack water, even in bright sunlight.
However, once the tide has begun a healthy rise, the action can
turn from ice-cold to red-hot. This is also true with specks,
should you be seeking to set in your winter stash of skillet material. Point is, work the tides—slack low or low and barely rising
on the flats, the other forms of benthic structure otherwise. And
don't let a lack of action get you disgusted and cause you to head
home too soon. Things change quickly during winter!

Some of the structure mentioned in the above paragraph
would be best described as junk, and its presence varies by location. (Please recall Hell Hole #1 in Chapter 4, which shall be
summoned back into existence shortly for reference.) But no
matter where you are fortunate enough to find some of it (yeah,
fortunate—*very* fortunate!), you may have located a spot for the

ages! Since a large percentage of my winter-caught reds came from such structure, I feel obliged to expound on it a bit.

Reds will usually hold to a very specific part of a "junk pile," especially during winter. Therefore, anything fitting the description should be worked very thoroughly—and *very slowly*. Gear should be on the stout side, and a popping rig with its jig sweetened a bit is recommended. Granted, in reasonably clear water, straight-up jigs and even spinnerbaits will work well, but the tackle best suited for their use will probably be a bit too flimsy to hold up to a double-digit fish's surge into the structure. Stick with the popping rig, and if at all possible, fish it while on the trolling motor. In other words, do *not* set the anchor! That, in case you've forgotten, will allow you a quick escape to "safe" water—safer, anyway.

Sadly, junk piles are not nearly as common in many areas as they once were. I guess that's best for the environment, but I, at least, could sure use a couple more in my life. If you find a good one, keep it under your hat!

Although winter's shallow reds do warm up a bit during the best times to fish for them, they can still be sluggish. Therefore slow retrieves are best. However, slow retrieves over oyster beds and other such "foul grounds" can result in all too frequent hang-ups. There are two ways to lessen that potential.

The first is to use a popping rig. In most instances, suspending the jig between 2 and 3 feet beneath the float will prevent most snags but still allow the jig to be worked near enough to bottom to get the fish's attention. Popping the float sharply every five seconds or thereabouts—and not dragging it back toward you during the pauses—will give the fish time to locate the jig.

The second way is to use the lightest jig you can cast and feel on the retrieve in whatever wind is blowing. In fairly light airs, I will try to fly-fish with Clouser Minnow–type patterns—which permit a very slow retrieve—or casting $\frac{1}{8}$-ounce jig-heads. The popping rig is used in windier conditions or when I have to use a sweetener to provide additional appeal for coping with some grungy water.

Reds—which don't seem to mind any cold above 45 degrees or thereabouts—often compel me to work a Dog or fly-rod popper across shallow oysters, submerged points, flats, and such. When doing so I always keep an eye out for a visible target. Spotting them hereabouts isn't as easy as it becomes later on when the sun gets higher in the sky, but it is possible. And need I say that watching a 10-pound red blow up on a surface lure will take the chill out of your bones in a hurry, even if it isn't your first fish of the year? Walking a slow dog is usually the best retrieve.

I have no doubt that many readers who make midwinter fishing trips to the coast will continue to concentrate their efforts on the depths; after all, it's "tradition." I also have no doubt that many of them will make respectable catches doing so. These lines were created to inform them that, contrary to popular opinion, all the fish in the estuary are assuredly *not* ganged up in the deep holes. At least, they aren't during normal winter weather, and that includes occasional light freezes.

And those fish that remain shallow are well worth a directed effort. So are the ones that associate with piers and docking areas.

Throughout much of my adult life, piers have contributed greatly to the net worth of my freezer's contents during winter. Until quite recently, though, those assets were almost always acquired after dark and from specks. However, not long ago some market studies (i.e., fishing trips) resulted in previously unrealized profits in (A) the sources of the aforementioned assets (i.e., fillets); (B) the time in which the sources of said assets were most profitably traded (i.e., caught); and the practices (i.e., patterns) that were involved in gaining those profits. And I avow that if someone ever accuses you of utilizing insider information by applying the following data to your trading in this market, those accusations will be coming from someone who wasn't paying any attention to this!

I wouldn't say it all began on that raw Christmas Eve afternoon in 2004, but the day's miserable weather played an important part in it—thick clouds spitting sleet, 37 degrees, and a rather brisk 15-knot northerly with conditions forecast to deteriorate. On a whim—perhaps just to see if I still "had it"—I bundled up, unlimbered a casting rod, and, armed with a small box of light jigs, drove over to a nearby marina. There, while walking along two of its five piers, I jigged up eight reds in the short time before I began fearing for my freezing fingers. Granted, most of the fish were rats, but catching them sure beat the heck out of staying home watching Molly Poly vs. Timid Tech in the Hardhead Bowl on TV!

The next day, a major snowstorm smothered much of the Southeast, creating absurd conditions for the annual drive from home to my daughter's house halfway across the state to celebrate Christmas with the kids and grandsons. And I must confess that because of all the detours due to the snow and iced-up roads, I saw places I had never seen before and devoutly pray I will never see again! But all that aside, we made it there and back again alive, and on the 29th with the sun out and the temperature at a balmy 63 degrees, I sortied to the marina again. There, during bright midday, I released a half dozen reds and sacked two frying-size flounders!

By that time, it had become fairly obvious that reds and a few flounders, if no specks, could be caught from piers during winter daylight hours. Admittedly, that's about all my market research revealed on that nasty Christmas Eve afternoon (except that "the stupid factor"—a lifelong malady that led to such extreme behavior—still ran freely through my blood). However, the trip on the 29th resulted in some very profitable data.

That was based on an adjustment of sorts that I had made a while back to my nighttime speck-trading practices. Historically, those were to initially cast a fairly light jig across the edges of a pier's lighted water, then allow it to sink near bottom, and then to retrieve it slowly—a very profitable practice. Still, there had been times when trading was slow, and some very interesting commotion was taking place in the dark water directly beneath the pier, even on some pretty cold nights. Eventually the racket demanded that my normal practice be adjusted to vertically jigging right alongside the piers. And throughout that winter, that technique turned out to be at least as profitable as casting, and it even produced fish in the darker water some distance from the lights' glow! Also, on numerous nights later that winter that often required insulated coveralls for a degree of comfort, it produced reds from the top 2 feet of the very dark water column.

While all that was quite enlightening, the very profitable data I acquired on 29 December 2004 was the result of deep vertical jigging during daylight, "deep" being about 6 feet: most fish were caught along the shaded side of the pier, not on the sunlit side where the water might have been a tad bit warmer. And the "shaded side" part of future trading became a steadfast procedure for targeting reds and flounders.

Nevertheless, initially there was a minor glitch in the program. If I walked along a pier in a certain direction, my shadow would pass over the water that I intended to speculate before I could trade. I have no clue whether or not the fish noticed my shadow's movement and were turned off by it, but when I fished in water that had just been affected by my shadow, I didn't catch anything. A much more profitable procedure was to walk past the part of the pier where I intended to trade in such a manner as to keep my shadow off the water, then retrace my steps while I traded. This kept my shadow behind me—and I caught fish like that.

So the fish were holding to the shaded side of the piers. This led to the thought that visibility near bottom there might be rather limited, even though the water was quite clear throughout most of the entire trading period. That soon inspired the idea that profits might be increased by enhancing the lure in such a way that would allow the fish to detect it more easily. With natural baits being an unacceptable option, I shortly made a raid on my ultralight freshwater box and procured a couple of $\frac{1}{8}$-ounce, lipless crankbaits with rattles.

And I am pleased to report that I caught a fair number of rat reds and frying-size flounders on them while vertically jigging them with short, sharp jerks along the shaded edges of the piers (and, incidentally, also at night). But I was not at all impressed with their profit margins, as they cost much more than my jigs did, and I soon lost both of them to bottom rubble. Still, vertically jigging a Tiny Rat-L-Trap along a pier does work for reds, et al., during winter.

That said, the realization that a rattling jig should be much more profitable than a silent one (Or a 'Trap) soon arose. So did a rather hostile bid: how to make a jig rattle. Nevertheless, the buyout was thwarted after I had destroyed only a meager handful of heads and various grubs while attempting the modification, and again I was quite happy with the results.

There are three important factors in the lightweight rattling jig. The first is a $\frac{1}{8}$-ounce, round jig-head with a size 1/0 short-shank hook. This is threaded through a 3-inch shad-type grub. (Clear chartreuse with glitter or pearl with a black back is a good choice and is available, as are the jig-heads, at Wal-Mart.) The key is to thread the hook through the grub in such a way as to leave as much room as possible in the grub's "belly." And mind you, this works effectively only with a shad-type grub.

The third factor leads to the equivalent of a stock split. Drive over to your friendly Academy Sporting Goods store. (If those aren't present in your area, you may have to place an order with Bass Pro Shops.) Purchase two cards of Excalibur EWR4 worm rattles. They run around $2.50 per card of 10, and you will need the extras, I promise! Back at home now, carefully insert a rattle, pointed end first, into the front of the grub as close to the bottom of the hook as possible. (The grub's deep belly allows this.) Push it firmly all the way into the grub—otherwise it will work its way out. Vertically jig it with slowly-paced, short but sharp jerks just off bottom—day or night.

Besides accounting for more reds and many more flounders than I ever caught from a pier during a single winter, the rattling jig produced numerous specks, including my largest of 2005, toward winter's end. The day I caught that one, some excessive computer work had just about driven me to the point where I was about to sell some bullish stock short and decided that before I crashed and burned I'd better take a break. Instead of heading for the local coffee-and-socializing shop, though, I took a casting rod over to the marina. And I avow that a short fishing (and catching) break is a much better cure for computer burnout (and for cabin fever) than coffee-shop socializing!

So if you know of such a place, get permission to fish there from the overseer, and the next time you need to escape—night or day—bundle up, gather your casting rod and a box of rattle-enhanced jigs, and try some wintertime redfish/flounder/speck speculating. You could be shocked at what you've been missing.

IV

Tackle and Techniques

CHAPTER 13

Fine Points

It wasn't really all that long ago when the comparatively few folks who actually fished for redfish used pretty stout tackle. More recently, a few of the guides who began to emerge from these waters advertised the use of "light tackle" as a draw for customers and, compared to what had been used in the past, it did allow the fish to cut up a bit more and therefore provided an enjoyable change and a degree of excitement to the uneducated masses. These days, however, one can see that some of that "light" tackle was pretty heavy.

I confess to having used a Penn International 30 loaded with a quarter mile or so of 50-pound Dacron on a few of my initial forays after bulls—thought I was really doing it right, too! Not long thereafter, though, I dropped down to a beefy, 6½-foot casting rod and an Ambassadeur 7000 loaded with 30-pound mono, then 20-pound, for the same purpose, and basically that's about the caliber of the guns I presently hunt them with. A rowdy surf and its required heavy weights, though, will demand longer, heavier rods and stronger line—on either a casting or a spinning reel. On the other hand, I have used—and still use—some pretty light gear in inshore waters, some of which might have been a little too light.

Excluding the varied and sundry fly-fishing outfits with which I have sought inshore reds for many decades, the gear I have used within that time has been fairly consistent in nature—well, with a couple of exceptions. Two outfits were standards of sorts throughout the period: a 6½-foot, fairly whippy popping rod and a 6-foot, straight-gripped and fairly stiff ("fast") casting rod that I believe was intended for freshwater fishing with plastic worms. Both were complemented with high-end casting reels holding around 150 yards of 17-pound for the popping rod and 14-pound for the shorter one. Those covered almost all the bases, and I must declare that when given a tiny amount of care, high-end reels will perform very nicely for a *long* time. They are well worth the dollars!

Why not use spinning gear? Years ago I did, discovered that it generally sucked, and that was that. Actually, I never felt that a spinning outfit offered the "feel" that a casting rod does. Whatever, a lot of folks must like 'em, so it's your choice there.

I think I'll leave that paragraph where it is, but just about the time I finished writing it, I recalled a time when I did use—and quite avidly—an ultralight spinning outfit for reds. Tried the same type gear for fly fishing, too—4-pound stuff. And though I caught a number of good fish with both—and broke off only a very few, I felt the rather long fights were overstressing the fish that I intended to release. Most assuredly it was great fun, but . . .

Anyway, now I feel a tale coming on.

I had been very successfully tossing Pet 13 spoons at skinny-water reds with the little outfit for some time and eventually related the fact to a guy I occasionally fished with. He apparently thought it sounded like something that might add a little spark to his daily redfishing, bought a comparable outfit, and shortly thereafter mentioned that his first trip with it was pure delight!

On our first trip together not long thereafter, we were confronted with some chilly and rather grungy water, so I unlimbered my popping rod and began prospecting a baited rig with it. My friend broke out his new toy, rigged it up similarly—much to my dismay—and proceeded to hook a nice red which he commenced to winch in without much fanfare. After scrutinizing the little outfit—and it truly was an ultralight one—I asked him what the rating of his line was. It was 14-pound, he answered. Oh . . .

There sure aren't any rules to dictate what kind of tackle a guy should use to catch reds, but if he decides to fish ultralight, he should fish ultralight all the way. Well, shouldn't he?

Perhaps not—whatever trips your trigger, I've always said. Anyway, not long after that I decided to speculate a rather wimpy 4-weight fly rod, size 4 flies, and a 4-pound leader. And the fish I caught—some nice ones, too—ended up in the cooler, so they had more problems to contend with than being overly stressed from what might have been an extended contest.

A buddy and I sally forth to do battle with the spot-tailed beasts on fly tackle. We catch a few, then I offer him my 4-weight rod, clearly informing him that's precisely what it is. He nods in apparent understanding and then proceeds to hook a good fish, plants the steel in its lip, and then initiates a rather forceful attempt to prevent it from reaching the grass.

Pop!

He said that one of my knots must have been bad. I said he was awfully heavy-handed with that 4-pound leader. "Four-pound?" he inquired?

"Well, what the hell else do you expect to find on a wimpy 4-weight fly rod?" I responded—or something very close to that. Whatever, I guess if you offer a friend your ultralight rod, you should inform him that it's ultralight all the way and not simply hope he realizes it.

Not long thereafter, I kicked the ultralight habit, and these days I'm glad I did. During the warm months especially, reds can get stressed to the point of being life-threatened during an extended conflict, and I sure don't want to contribute to that. Besides, it's rather hard to work a Dog—or a size 1/0 popper—with ultralight gear!

And the Dog brings up a fine point. Several folks I know swear and be damned that long, rather whippy rods are best for working the big topwaters. Not I! That 6-foot, "fast" casting rod gives me the feel to know that the fish has actually eaten the lure and not just made a rowdy pass at it. All that give in a whippy stick may mask that feel just long enough for the fish to return your lure without being attached to it.

Also, when working jigs deep in current, that rod is also preferred for the "feel factor," and on winter pier-fishing trips I even use a shorter one, though still a rather fast one. It has superb feel! Point is, short, fast sticks offer advantages you should consider. Take all the help you can get!

Same thing goes for the reels, both spinning and casting models. In case you don't realize it, those come with gizmos on them that regulate the tension on the spool, which in turn hinders the progress of a fish moving in a general direction away from you. These are referred to as "drags," and if you look up the definition of the word—either on Google or in your trusty dictionary, it matters not—you will find that it refers to something that hinders, not stops, a particular forward progress. When found on fishing reels, drags are intended to slow the fish, *not* to stop it. So set the drag so that the line can still be pulled from the reel, but at a hindering pace. Almost always, that does not require the drag to be "sundowned," yet you would not believe the number of anglers I have seen fishing with their reels' drags screwed down to such a point. That's the best way I know to break off a good red!

And on that note, *always* back the drag all the way off at the end of the day. It will last a lot longer—and run a lot smoother—that way.

That has to do with maintenance, so here's something else along that line. Some folks insist on spraying their gear down after a trip with fresh water from a hose and a nozzle. Washing the salt off a rod like that is okay, I guess, but never do it to a reel. That will force grit, sand, and salt into the reel's inner workings and possibly cause more damage than just leaving the salt water inside it. Fact is, when I am fishing brackish or up-country areas, I "wash" my reels about every four months or so. Maybe a bit more often than that, but not much! Whatever the case, no matter how often you clean your reels, to do so, first remove them from the rod, then *soak* them in fresh water for 15 minutes or thereabouts, gently sloshing them around a bit from time to time and ensuring there is absolutely no soap—like as in *none!*—in the water. Then shake out the excess, remount the reel on the rod, and it will be all dried out and ready to slay reds by the beginning of the next day's trip. Again—and I could care less what that guide or deckhand does, *never* spray a reel to clean it! Got that?

How about all that hullabaloo about changing your line twice a year? That's fine if you have plenty of time and money and don't have anything better to do with it. I usually whack the leader and 2 or 3 feet of line after a trip on general principles, then tie on a fresh leader. Also, if I've had a long-distance runner that might have dinged some line on oysters or grass, I'll cut out a lot of it. But I don't arbitrarily replace all the line on a reel whenever someone has said I ought to—usually only when its diameter on the spool begins to look a little small, and over the years that has apparently been often enough. Regularly scheduled line changing is an attempt by the line companies to sell more of their product!

So is fluorocarbon that comes on 150-yard "reel-filler" spools. Fluorocarbon is leader material, man! Still, 150 yards of 20-pound for 10 bucks or thereabouts is pretty cheap leader material, especially considering that it's fluorocarbon. I used a

Reds of all sizes have no aversion to striking a surface lure!

spool of it for five years and still had a while to go before the suggested expiration date. Never had a bit of trouble with it, either.

One thing about fluorocarbon, though—well, actually two. The first is to slobber all over the knot connecting it to mono before you draw the knot tight. Water doesn't work, spit does, and plenty of spit works best of all! Also, fluorocarbon works okay with topwaters such as Dogs, but don't use it with fly-rod poppers. That's because it sinks pretty fast, and that can adversely affect the pop-ability of the popper, especially in the heavier strengths. Use mono for poppers, fluorocarbon for all other enticers—when you don't need wire.

Let's see—hooks. I simply cannot bring myself to fish for reds using barbless hooks or even smash the barbs down with pliers. However, some hooks have pretty obtrusive barbs—thick, heavy, and extending into the hook's gap much farther than I feel is necessary. I remove almost all those barbs with a small flat file, leaving only a trace of one above the hook's point. The main purpose in doing this is to facilitate setting the hook—it goes in easier without all that barb—and once it's set, it will still hold securely.

But not as securely as it would have had I not filed down the barb! So removing it is easier on the fish as well as on me when I have to remove it from a human extremity, should it have ended up somewhere it shouldn't have.

A few folks I know—all of them fly-fishing guides—refuse to let a client fish without first flattening the barbs on their flies—a strategic maneuver intended for self-preservation. That might seem to be somewhat extreme, but some folks are rather averse to removing a hook from someone else, and at times that hook can be planted in such a place that it's quite difficult for the hooked party to remove it himself. If its barb has been smashed, the hook comes out (of the guide) a *lot* easier, so for your sake, your companions' sakes, and the fish's sake, file down those barbs a bit.

One final note here. I have not mentioned the use of spoons very often in these pages, but in places they are very effective lures for reds. One of those is in and around the surf, where both bulls and regular reds can be taken on them. The only drawback to using them is they will twist your line badly, and snap swivels used to connect them to the line for the purpose of preventing that can be opened inadvertently by a fish that has taken the spoon deep within its throat.

To prevent that, install a #5 stainless steel split ring to the line eye of the spoon—or replace whatever is there with one. Now add a small but still appropriately strong barrel swivel to the split ring, and tie the leader to that. This simple modification greatly lessens line twist and—to me—is more effective than rigging the spoon on a short fish-finder of sorts without a weight (i.e., slick line, swivel, leader, and spoon).

Also, especially if you fish a lot while wading, you may want to consider replacing a spoon's treble hook with a single hook. That way you won't get one of those extra points in your finger while you are unhooking a fish. For a $\frac{1}{2}$-ounce model, try the size 1 or 1/0 stainless steel, short-shank Mustad C68S SS. It's a good one—sharp and with a very small barb that you really don't need to smash.

On that note, you'll need one of those pairs of $149.95 titanium pliers. *Not!* Wal-Mart offers a long long-nosed, stainless type that is excellent for smashing barbs and retrieving hooks and only costs around 10 bucks. I've had three and lost two of them overboard—imagine that happening to a couple of those absurdly priced versions.

CHAPTER 14

Weights and Baits

N ow don't get all bent out of shape about what follows—there is a purpose for it!

Back in 1976, I got a severe itch to catch a tarpon and, in an obsessive attempt to scratch it, bought a boat and three high-dollar trolling outfits specifically for that purpose. Then I spent a good part of the next five summers trolling and casting outlandishly large spoons around some offshore waters that had for years been fairly well known for producing them—and never caught the first one! Oh, I caught plenty of jacks—and sharks—and a few king mackerel, and I did jump off a handful of the great silver beasts, but it took quite a while for me to figure out that something just wasn't quite right with my presentation. After a trip with a couple of guys who really knew their stuff, I got the feeling that perhaps my spoons weren't working deeply enough.

So I decided to weight one of them. And I did know just

enough about the physics of the matter to realize that a heavy weight jerking about wildly on the line above the spoon with each of a tarpon's jumps would surely lead to the fish's loss. So I tied the weight—an 8-ounce swivel sinker—to the swivel between line and leader with a short length of 20-pound mono. That is called a "break-away system" in some circles, and I mentioned it in Chapter 13 as an option for bottom fishing for bull reds near a jetty. And one fine July afternoon in 1981, the technique fulfilled its purpose with the "poons," sinking the spoon much deeper than it would run unweighted and then breaking free with the first jump of a 7-foot tarpon. And that one stayed hooked!

I relate that unrelated incident to illustrate that in saltwater fishing it is quite possible that the only thing more important than using the best lures and baits is putting them where the fish can detect them. In most cases—the incident with the tarpon being an exception, but still illustrating the effective use of weights—"properly weighted" signifies the lightest weight that will get the intended job done. It also implies using the right type of weight for that job.

Although the incident with the tarpon was undoubtedly the most extreme example of the effective weighting of an enticer for any species in my entire saltwater fishing career, the truth is I could have probably used several types and sizes of weights (i.e., spark plugs?) to sink my spoon on that memorable July afternoon. However, you must realize that at the time, I was grasping at straws trying to discover some way—any way!—to get the spoon a little bit deeper. In most other scenarios, the requirements are a bit more definitive.

For example, you are fishing for bull reds alongside a jetty made of boulders. You want your bait on bottom, but you know that sooner or later your sinker will foul in the rocks. Therefore, you also want to keep your losses to a minimum. What's the solution?

One is related in Chapter 13, and it does work! Another, which I mentioned that I don't care for but which is reputed to

Many minor adjustments—like adding a split-ring and swivel directly to a spoon—can make a big difference in your successes.

also be effective, is to use a three-way swivel with the line tied to one eye, the heavier leader to another, and the lighter sinker-dropper to the third. That, like the breakaway sinker attached to the barrel swivel as I prefer, will (or should!) lead to the loss of only the sinker when it fouls in the rocks.

Bottom fishing over sand is a bit different, and the best terminal rig is usually determined by sea conditions. In calm water with minimal current, a fish-finder is a good choice. In my humble opinion, that does not include the little sleeve with a dropper eye on it that you may have seen advertised. (You thread the line through the sleeve, tie it to the leader swivel, and tie the sinker dropper to the eye.) Personally, I don't want anything like that sliding up and down my line and slamming into the swivel; a lead egg sinker sliding up and down my line (and occasionally slamming into the swivel) has caused me absolutely no problems over many years, and I do not intend to fix something that ain't broke!

Some of the best action to be had with bull redfish can take place in some pretty nasty conditions. I quit "enjoying" that kind of foolishness about the time I turned 50, but I still fish on days when the swells or the current can prevent the egg sinker on my fish-finder from staying put. When that happens, another "three-way rig" is in order.

Liking three-way swivels about as much as those sliding-sleeve gizmos, I again tie my line to one end of a black barrel swivel, and about 3 feet of 50-pound fluorocarbon to the other end of the swivel and to the ever-present size 8/0 circle hook. Then I take a pyramid sinker—beginning with the same weight as the last egg sinker that wouldn't hold bottom—and tie it to the line end of the swivel with a foot of 30-pound mono. If that won't stay where I want it to, I'll progress upwards to 12 ounces or a bit more, and if that still won't stay put, then it's probably getting too rough for me to be out there anyway!

One thing. The heavier the weight you use, the more likely it becomes that its resistance will alert a red that something has varied from the natural order of things. That's one of the main reasons to use the lightest weight that will do the job.

On a slightly more quiescent theme, I have some up-country friends who come south once or twice every winter to do some inshore fishing. Typically at the time, the reds are found along the shoreline drop-offs of canals and tidal cuts, and popping shrimp-tipped jigs for them in that particular setting has been consistently productive for me for well over three decades. The rig is a ¼-ounce jig suspended beneath a 3-inch weighted popping cork on 2 to 3 feet of 30-pound fluorocarbon. You cast it tightly against the shoreline, and as you work it out and the water depth suddenly exceeds the length of the dropper, the weight of the jig will cause the cork to abruptly sit upright and slightly deeper in the water. That point is usually the strike zone, so the rig, besides catching fish, also serves to show you where they should be. It's a great prospecting rig in somewhat chilly or off-color water, and the dropper can be lengthened another foot or so if necessary without losing any of the rig's effectiveness.

Last winter, my buddies came down armed with what someone had told them was an improvement. Similarly to my rig, they had first tied their lines to a small barrel swivel. Then they tied a foot or so of slightly heavier mono "spacer" to the other end of that swivel and ran it through the float's stem, which had previously been superglued to the inside of the float. However, here's where it began to differ. Next they threaded a $\frac{1}{4}$-ounce egg sinker onto the spacer below the float and tied the spacer to another swivel. The rig was then completed with around $1\frac{1}{2}$ feet of leader tied to the other end of that swivel and to a Kahle hook.

Once they had retrieved this rig to the point where the egg sinker came off bottom—that being in very shallow water, there was no way they could tell any further change in the water's depth, since there was no weight on the end of their terminal assembly to affect the attitude of the cork. Yeah, they caught fish—it was a good thing, though, that there were so many around that winter! I caught many more, with much less effort, on my ole faithful rig where the telltale weight was at its bottom end. Take all the help you can get!

Incidentally, after that trip I never saw the "improvement" in use again.

The old faithful popping rig is fairly easy to cast, and that's an important consideration when casting a bait or baited jig, not simply dropping it overboard or trolling it. These days there are a number of rigs that mimic that old standby, and I would be lying if I didn't believe that they evolved—at least in some degree—because of my writings about the one I was using so effectively so long ago. And it wasn't my idea! Fact is, I'm not so sure it was originated by the guy who first showed it to me—my redfish-stomping buddy and dear old family friend Ralph Chastain, now of Lookout Mountain, Georgia. But whatever, they all work pretty well—I'm just a bit partial to my old standard.

Finally, if you are fishing jigs and find yourself without one that is heavy enough for your purposes, you can make one that will suffice well enough. Take a swivel sinker of the necessary weight and cut and remove the swivel with wire cutters. Next, fasten a single hook of your desired size to a leader, slide the sinker—then an appropriately sized crimping sleeve—down the leader to the hook, and anchor the sinker in place there by lightly crimping the sleeve to the leader just above it. Then attach the leader to the line—your choice of methods—and finish off your "jig" with a soft plastic, the size and type again dependent on your preference. It all may not look very appealing to you, but it will wiggle nicely as you jig it at some depth or retrieve it after a cast. And to me, any jig, no matter how ugly it is, is easier to work and retain the feel of than any fish-finder rig, which must suffice in such a situation unless you create your own jig. I have taken a number of reds (and two tarpon) on these creations, and they were pretty ugly, but the type *will* get you out of a jam!

So will the act of properly weighting all your "baits."

And there are a lot of those that will suffice if you are unable to acquire an adequate number of mullet heads—or if you are fishing inshore for juvenile fish. Fact is, in my opinion a redfish is second only to a cobia in the indiscretion of its diet. So sit back and relax, and I will tell you a tale of redfish groceries.

Penaeid shrimp, various killifish, and numerous types of crabs typically make up a good part of a juvenile redfish's normal diet and are commonly used as enticers by fishermen. It's also no secret that half a blue crab worked on a fish-finder rig in the surf or on the bottom of a pass is a top producer of bulls. But other types of crabs apparently have great appeal, even to smaller inshore fish.

I was once easing along a shallow, narrow tidal cut on an almost dead-low, high-summer tide. The adjacent marsh was dry—well, exposed mud, and fiddler crabs were scurrying here and there all over it. One apparently got too close to the edge of the cut—and really quite nearby to me—and an unnoticed red launched itself at it and in the process grounded itself on the mud. I actually could have scooped the fish up in my landing net! However, having already acquired enough skillet material for the day, I was content to watch the fish kick its way back into the water. It was quite entertaining—and you should have seen those fiddler crabs scatter!

Another rather surprising revelation was the result of two pretty big reds I caught one spring morning way back in some up-country marsh. Both were in the 11- to 12-pound range, and each one had a common eel about a foot long in its stomach. And they were still hungry enough (greedy enough?) to eat my shrimp-tipped jig!

Then there was the 18-inch red I caught on a little jig while fishing from a pier one late winter day. I would have released it, but it was built more like a tuna than a red. That's because further inspection led to the recovery of the 6-inch mullet it had recently eaten. And I measured both the red and the mullet for the sake of scientific accuracy. That was another greedy fish! And you think that a Top Dog is too big for redfish? Whatever, reds just might eat for the fun of it—like some folks I know.

Always seeking to pass the time profitably, one spring I decided to run some trotlines in some local brackish marsh. The cuts that laced it had shown plenty of evidence that they held some creditable blue catfish—friends and I had even caught a few of them on our baited popping rigs while fishing for reds during the winter months. So one spring evening, I set three lines with a dozen or so hooks apiece and baited them with crawfish that I had picked up while they were crossing the road the previous evening. The next afternoon showed that no catfish had eaten my crawfish baits, but several nice reds had! After the same thing happened the next night, I decided that I would much prefer catching my reds on a rod and therefore began baiting my lines with chunks of rabbit that a friend had shot the previous winter. Turned out that was a pretty good waste of prime rabbit meat—but at least I didn't catch any more reds on my trotlines!

Speaking of trotlines, in the days when redfish were commercial targets in areas where that is no longer permitted, I would occasionally come across such a line stretched low across the water's surface and barely visible until you were almost on it as you sped across the flats in an effort to prevent your boat from being grounded. Frequently, yellow or green penny balloons—the long, skinny kind—set to flick the surface ripples were employed as lures. And they worked!

One morning I unintentionally got too close to one of those lines to avoid it, and while I was picking the hooks out of my shirt I noticed one of them was "baited" with an oleander leaf. No kidding! And after I rid myself of the slight inconveniences, I ran the line a ways and discovered a red that had been hooked on such a bait. All I can say about that is that the line's owner was sure cutting his operating costs. Oleander leaves!

I may have mentioned the possibility of reds eating small bass in up-country areas. That is entirely speculative, but I know for sure that they will eat pygmy sunfish—referred to in some locales as "ditch minnows"—in those waters. I've found reds so full of them—and still eating them—that they were regurgitating them while they ate. That's definitely some greedy fish! Whatever, where they are found, ditch minnows make excellent redfish enticers and can be gathered—from ditches containing generally fresh water—in standard minnow traps baited with chunks of French bread or freshly boiled shrimp heads.

Add to that threadfin shad, cigar minnows, squid, cut baits from several sources—ladyfish being a particularly effective one—plastic worms, rattling crankbaits, tiny tube jigs, all sorts of flies intended for both saltwater and freshwater purposes, and probably varied and sundry other odds and ends with which I have caught reds on occasion but have temporarily forgotten, and the point should have been made. And that is: "If you aren't catching redfish, change spots, not baits."

That works a lot more often than it doesn't.

CHAPTER 15

Pitching Plastic

When my wife Barbara and I moved to the Mississippi River Delta back in 1968, my fishing equipment consisted of two casting outfits, one spinning rig, two fly rods and reels, a small fly box, and one tackle box that contained mostly spinnerbaits, crankbaits, and surface lures intended for largemouth bass.

The number of rods and reels of all types that littered my loft prior to Hurricane Katrina is not especially relevant, and I see no need to relate how many tackle boxes lined one of its walls. But what is noteworthy is the fact that at least half the contents of five of those boxes were made up of soft plastics. Believe me, the racks in the sporting goods sections of Wal-Mart did not come even close to holding the numbers, sizes, shapes, and colors that once comprised my stash of those lures! Well, figuratively speaking, anyway. But why did I amass such a collection? Because they worked—and for literally every creature that I fished for, both in fresh and salt water.

But back in the late 1960s, there was no opportunity to acquire such a plethora of plastic. Very little was available, so when we discovered their productivity we salty types were limited to purchasing what there was, or to cutting 6-inch freshwater "bass worms" in half and then threading them on a $\frac{1}{4}$-ounce or so jig-head. Both worked—to some degree, anyway, but it didn't take long for the plastic people to realize the genre's potential and to make a few improvements—and a lot of variations—in them. Soft plastics have come a long way, baby, to improve the results of our fishing efforts—or have they, like so many other things, been designed to appeal to us first (spell that M-A-K-E M-O-N-E-Y) and to the fish second? Let's see . . .

The first soft plastics I used in salt water were pink, in the neighborhood of 3 inches long, and looked exactly like the 3-inch head section of a 6-inch worm. They had neither built-in action nor built-in scent, yet they caught redfish galore—as well as specks and flounders—when retrieved either directly or beneath a popping cork. So did the "shrimp tails" that appeared shortly thereafter. Individuals of both types, incidentally, typically held up to several fish.

Nowadays when a fish bites the aft end off of a "wiggle-tail grub," we immediately discard it and thread a new one onto the jig-head—and the manufacturers smile once again. I do too when another fish quickly belts the new one, but occasionally I also think of the actionless "worm halves" of yesteryear and wonder what might have happened if I had continued fishing with the tailless grub. But that would be foolish, considering the advantage of the fish-appealing wiggle that enhances many of today's soft plastics.

In truth, these lures—when they are intact—can work so well that a guy could reach into a bin containing all sorts of different types, sizes, and colors, close his eyes, and grab a handful of them, and probably catch reds with them the next time he went fishing! But there are some considerations—and a few adjustments—to be made to get the best out of them.

Once I discovered that skirted spinnerbaits and buzzbaits were as effective on redfish as they were on bass, I used them extensively in the bays, ponds, and tidal cuts around my new home for over a decade. The skirts, however, proved to be a real pain in the butt, either becoming mangled in short order by redfish teeth or turning into gooey, useless blobs between trips. And spare skirts were very hard to come by locally. On the other hand, soft plastic "minnows" were becoming readily available, they cost less than a skirt, and they proved to be equally if not more effective on both spinnerbaits and buzzbaits. I prefer the $2\frac{1}{2}$-inch "junior" sizes for both applications. Those fit the skirt retainers found on the buzzbaits' heads very well, and they are made to order for the type of jig-head I like best for reds, both for serving straight up and for creating spinnerbaits: the $\frac{1}{8}$- or $\frac{1}{4}$-ounce, round-headed models with short-shank, heavy-wire hooks in Nos. 1/0 and 2/0. Now here are a couple of helpful hints that should make life a little easier for you, both when you dress your jig-head with the soft plastic tail and when you are fishing with it. And they apply to straight-up jigs as well as to spinnerbaits and buzzbaits.

The "tail keepers" on jig-heads and the skirt-keepers on buzzbaits are round; the soft plastic "minnows"—and many other styles—are basically oval. Therefore, if you misalign the tail slightly as you thread it onto the keeper, the keeper can tear through the side of the tail. That may not reduce the lure's effectiveness, but it will weaken the connection, allowing short strikes to pull the tail from the keeper. To prevent this, slightly flatten the keeper vertically with pliers.

Now thread the tail onto the hook, but just before you push it onto the keeper, put a drop of superglue there. Then quickly push the tail onto the keeper. The manufacturers do not approve of that procedure, but it will keep you fishing more and replacing tails less.

Just don't use too much superglue, or it will eat up the plastic tail!

Once you seat the tail onto the keeper it should be perfectly straight, not curved upward or bunched up between the bend of the hook and the lure's head. If you discover the tail is somewhat askew, then allow the superglue to dry for about 30 seconds, grasp the tail on top of the keeper with one hand, and with the other hand gently pull the tail down and away from the bend of the hook. This will cause the tail to be torn slightly at the point where the hook emerges from it, but that won't hurt a thing once the superglue has set, and it will cause the tail to ride in a straight and natural fashion.

Plastics are highly effective lures for redfish.

While the minnow-type soft plastic works just fine on spinnerbaits and buzzbaits, in my opinion it does not wiggle as well as the "shad" type. This deeper-bodied, thinner, and more flexible model—and one which is admittedly more easily destroyed by fish—earns its keep on a bare jig-head.

Three scenarios come to mind where a straight-up jig/shad combo is hard to beat in the redfishing department. First is when it is suspended beneath a popping cork for shallow-water applications—and you can tip it with a shrimp if you so desire, though when the water's clarity permits it, I work mine unsweetened. By using the $\frac{1}{8}$-ounce jig-head previously discussed, you will get better action from the lure than if you used a heavier size. In this setting, the 3-inch shads are usually best.

The second scenario—if you have a thing for avoiding the use of spoons—is in the surf. Here, too, it is usually best to use the lightest jig-head you can cast and that will sink to bottom in any current and wave action that may be present. Seldom, though, have I encountered a fishable surf that required anything heavier than a $\frac{1}{4}$-ounce jig-head. Here, especially if bulls are about, 4-inch soft plastics are a good choice.

The third scenario, however—deep-jigging—is an entirely different matter. In places like the deltaic distributaries of coastal rivers, $\frac{3}{8}$- and even $\frac{1}{2}$-ounce heads are necessary to reach and hold the strike zone. The 3-inch variety of plastics is the best choice here—sweetened, if you so choose. Just remember that a piece of shrimp hooked onto the jig will increase the effects of the current that is acting on it and may not allow it to reach bottom where you want it to. In other words, if you sweeten your jig for prospecting in current, you may need to use one a little heavier than you would otherwise.

Then there's the subject of colors, and I freely confess that I had many more of those than I ever needed. That also puts smiles on the manufacturers' faces! Anyway, in most cases if a hungry red can locate a reasonably appealing lure, he will strike it, and soft plastics are most definitely reasonably appealing! Making it easy for him to locate one is the key, so here's a little rule of thumb for his benefit: light for light, dark for dark.

Consider "light" to be a sunny day with relatively shallow water—say, no more than 5 feet deep—with good clarity. Here, my steadfast choice of color is clear chartreuse with glitter. "Dark," on the other hand, would denote a cloudy sky, dingy water, and depth. In those conditions, black or purple have worked well. What about fishing 15 feet down in crystal-clear water on a cloudy day—or fishing in 2 feet of dingy water in bright sunlight? Who knows, but mixed lights and darks could be good reasons (excuses?) for having had so many colors in my tackle boxes!

Still, I'd bet if I threw away all the minnow and shad tails I owned that were not either clear chartreuse with glitter or purple, I would have still caught as many reds as I did. And if you like the ones that have their tail sections—or long, whippy dorsal fins—of contrasting colors, then go for it. Reds may care less, but you might discover an increase in the number of specks you catch.

I guess I should make some comments about soft plastics of a character other than shad or minnows, like the paddle-tailed and split-tailed types and long, thin "jerkbaits." Okay, why? In my most humble opinion, the paddle-tails are lifeless compared to a shad or minnow, though the split tails admittedly do okay under a popping cork and while being jigged vertically. Indeed, I have slayed some specks in that fashion but have taken very few reds on them and seldom use them now, since they, too, don't have as much built-in action as the wiggle-tails do—especially the shad types. And as far as jerkbaits go, I had a box full of them—from three different manufacturers in a half dozen different colors and in 4-inch and 4½-inch sizes—and never made a cast with any of them! They looked good, and several of my guide buddies swore by them. I guess I just kept forgetting I had them.

Maybe that was a good thing!

On the other hand, 4-inch, curly-tail grubs have served me well over many years in one specific setting: flipping for winter reds holding tightly to local manmade structure—boat-basin piers, rundown fishing camps, oil field odds and ends, and the like. Since the productive water there is typically less than 5 feet deep, and since this tactic, too, works best when the lure sinks slowly, use the lightest weight you can effectively flip. I normally Texas-rig the grub on a size 2/0 offset freshwater worm hook which is tied to about 6 inches of 30-pound mono "sinker spacer," which itself is tied to my 30-pound line. The ⅛-ounce bullet sinker I use most often is not pegged but allowed to slide up and down the 30-pound sinker spacer.

Admittedly, you could probably bait a jig with a shrimp, cast it to the spots I normally flip to, let it sink to bottom, and catch more reds than I do flipping my curly-tail grubs. But I'd bet a bundle again you wouldn't have as much fun as I do! Short-range flipping for reds is a real hoot—have I mentioned that before a time or two?

Oh, what color grub? Clear chartreuse with glitter, naturally. Hey, if it ain't broke, don't try to fix it!

Over the almost 40 years that I lived in the Delta, I caught reds almost every way imaginable—that was legal! So I guess it was part of the evolutionary process that eventually I tried "ultra-lighting" 'em. That was a blast, and the $1\frac{1}{2}$-inch shads that I used on $\frac{1}{16}$-ounce jig-heads were surprisingly effective, but the fad ran its course.

However, these days—especially during late winter and early spring—I have occasionally come across reds keying on small baitfish and rather reluctant to strike even a $2\frac{1}{2}$-inch shad. During those times, I have found that a 2-inch shad on a $\frac{1}{8}$-ounce, size 1 jig-head will often generate strikes. Since a lure that light is difficult at best to cast with my "spinnerbait stick," I worked it with a $5\frac{1}{4}$-foot, medium-light casting outfit (I built the rod out of a one-piece spinning rod blank and absolutely loved it!) and 8-pound line with a foot of 20-pound mono for a leader. That combination produced many reds without undue stress to them. It was really fun fishing, though if you try it, you may have to look on the freshwater side of the lure rack to find tails like those—crappie stuff. And it's likely you'll have to use them with appropriately sized spinning gear.

A lot of water has passed through the local marshes since I began fishing soft plastics for reds—and specks, and flounders, and stripers. And for tarpon, tripletail, and cobia, for that matter. These days—when I am not fly fishing, of course—you will seldom find any other type of lure tied to my line, and if you do, it will probably be a Dog.

But surface lures are fairly limited in their applications. Soft plastics, on the other hand—the different types and sizes and the accoutrements which further enhance their appeal—can be used successfully in literally every setting imaginable save that when the water is really grungy. Even then, you can tip 'em with a shrimp and often catch reds—been there/done that in turbid, chilly water for many winters. That just about covers all the bases, doesn't it?

The soft plastic manufacturers ought to like this chapter. Occasionally when a writer promotes a certain product, they send him a sample of that product as a token of their appreciation. (Very often, sales increase tremendously as a result of what's been written about a given product.) Well, I sure hope the soft plastic manufacturers don't do that because of this one; I've got way too many of them as it is! They'd probably send the wrong colors, anyway, and I sure don't need any more of those. Of course, you never can tell—I know a guy who swears by "strawberry," and since bass like "motor oil" worms, I don't see why redfish wouldn't like motor oil mullet! And 4-inch shads in "tuxedo" (black over pearl) sure work well on the bulls around my favorite jetty.

It's hard to beat a soft plastic for redfish . . .

CHAPTER 16

The Redoubtable Spinnerbait

S ince I have rather frequently mentioned spinnerbaits as effective producers of redfish, and other species, I feel that they deserve a separate chapter in these pages. At its conclusion—and for sure after you have seen for yourself!—I'm pretty sure you will agree.

Although I have caught a *lot* of redfish (and a *lot* of specks and flounders) over the years on spoons and various jigs, I have also been frequently chastened when a visible red showed no interest in them at all. It finally occurred to me that it was possible that the lures simply weren't being noticed, and after recalling some early successes with some sizable reds I had taken while working spinnerbaits in some local brackish marsh for largemouth bass— which I had assumed at the time were accidental—I decided to try them for reds in earnest. It paid off in big dividends!

This type of lure in the "in-line" fashion has been around for many years, the Snagless Sally being one of the originals. The "safety-pin" design made its appearance in the early 1950s, and the buzzbait a few years after that. All were initially intended for freshwater gamefish. Each is composed of a tail, either a shredded rubber or synthetic skirt, hair, or soft plastic minnow imitation, a wire shaft, and a revolving blade. And while the tail's wiggle and the blade's flash are characteristic of other types of lures, it is the vibration of the blade that sets the spinnerbait apart. It is so effective that I haven't slung a spoon in years and only use plain jigs either under a popping cork or when the fish are very deep. But it took a long time for other anglers to catch on, and only recently have I seen more than a few people using one for redfish. That's a shame, because they are missing out on one of the most productive lures to ever hit the salt.

The buzzbait—the most efficient shallow runner of the group—is constructed so that the bend of the shaft is in the same plane as the hook gap, making it reasonably weedless. The large, cupped blade creates a gurgling sound when retrieved slowly across the surface, and in shallow, grassy water it will call redfish better than a popping cork and will occasionally entice a good speck that somehow found its way into such waters.

The buzzbait—on which I have previously described my preferences—is indeed best utilized for reds in this particular setting. However, I recall a hot summer day when a buddy and I were fishing a shallow reef on a dingy, hard-falling tide. His shrimp-baited popping rig was accounting for some nice reds, but there were some good specks feeding on that reef, too, and they were reluctant to dig his jig out of the oysters. My buzzbait, on the other hand, met with their approval, and I supplemented my redfish limit with several very nice ones. All my friend caught was reds—and a few pesky sea catfish! Buzzbaits may be hard for some saltwater anglers to swallow, but they have their places and do a fine job.

And I must relate a tale about a place where they shouldn't have worked but they did, accounting for the only reds of the day—

though that might have been solely because I refused to speculate another lure. The place was a small, winding tidal cut some 4 to 5 feet deep and not quite far enough inside to be in the up-country, but pretty close. The fish—good ones in the 2-foot class and a bit larger—were holding to bottom in the middle of the cut, and I have no clue why I began working my buzzbait that deep! I could claim that there was junk on the bottom of that cut and I was using the buzzbait for its weedless properties, but I'd be lying. Sometimes, I guess, you just do stuff for the hell of it, and it works.

Whatever, no matter how flexible they may be, buzzbaits have a serious drawback, particularly when they are being used to target redfish, which regularly bend their rigid frames into semblances of drunken snakes. And after you (almost) straighten them out a time or two, they become very weak. While safety-pin spinnerbaits don't work as well in a buzzbait's intended setting, they work well enough, and they don't suffer from that particular disorder nearly as badly. They just aren't as much fun to work.

Safety-pin spinnerbaits have the broadest range of applications in the family of spinnerbaits and are attractive to popular creatures other than reds. These lures can be modified in so many ways that an attempt to describe them all would soon become quite boring. For simplicity's sake—and because it is so effective—I'll use my favorite as an illustration. It is created from a round $\frac{1}{8}$-ounce jighead with a heavy size 2/0 hook, a #3$\frac{1}{2}$ or #4 gold Hildebrandt safety-pin spinner—the smaller one being favored in ultraclear, shallow water, the larger one being used for everyday work—and the same type of grubtail I use on a buzzbait in chartreuse with glitter or in purple. In water depths from 1 to 4 or 5 feet and with reasonable clarity, this combination is awfully hard to beat.

Spinnerbaits of all types seem to work best when the fishing is done on the move with a bow-mounted trolling motor, thereby adhering to the basic tenet that in most cases the more water you cover, the more likely you will be to find fish. The spinnerbait permits this to be done much more efficiently than, say, a popping rig would, but one thing that must be remembered is that the lure's retrieve should not be too rapid. The freshwater term "slow-rolling" the blade is descriptive of what is often the best procedure for reds over oysters and along shoreline drop-offs deeper than, say, 3 feet. Work it just fast enough so that you can detect the spinner's vibrations, varying the lure's depth by the "countdown" method and the rod's position. In this manner, you can retrieve it at the same speed in various water depths. If that doesn't produce enough action for you, try a retrieve consisting of slow pumps and pauses—in effect "yo-yoing" the spinnerbait along bottom.

The spinnerbait could be the best all-around lure there is for reds in inshore waters.

And if that doesn't work, either try a Dog or go home!

Incidentally, that yo-yoing type of retrieve is often very effective when flounders might be encountered. Normally, these fish won't pursue a fast-moving lure very far, but the blade's vibration will alert the fish to its presence early on, and the slow, stop-and-go retrieve will allow the fish to run it down. Simply put, flounders will jump all over a well-presented spinnerbait.

And while I'm playing that song, so will larger-than-average specks! In clear water, where the splash of a popping cork often spooks them, or when dingy water prohibits the successful use of plugs or straight-up jigs, the spinnerbait falls right into place. My largest inshore speck, as well as another that was caught by a friend and was the biggest "inside" speck I had seen taken by anyone in many years, both struck spinnerbaits. So will stripers, in areas where they can be encountered. But redfish simply can't leave them alone.

The last variation of the spinnerbait is the in-line model, and though I used this type for only a short time, it bumped up my winter successes noticeably. Normal jig-heads are created with the hook's eye above the body. That won't work with an in-line spinner, since the blade can contact the eye, or even the jig-head, breaking up the vibrations. So I created my own heads by cutting the shafts of $\frac{1}{4}$-ounce buzzbaits just behind the line-tying eyes, thus removing all the bend in the shafts and the large cupped spinners. Then I constructed another "eye" in the shaft by twisting it with a pair of long-nosed pliers. To that eye I affixed a gold #$3\frac{1}{2}$ in-line spinner and topped it off with a soft plastic grub.

The configuration of this lure allowed it to get deeper quicker than the safety-pin type, and the flash and vibration often added just the right amount of enticement when, during winter, the fish—both reds and specks—were a little chilly and not in a serious feeding mood. It was best worked slowly—a 2-foot pull, then a drop-back, then another pull, maintaining contact at all times. It worked, and it is a viable option, but I no longer mess with it. Wrecked too many perfectly good buzzbaits in the process! Besides, these days find me fly fishing for reds most often—even in the depths of winter.

But I still fish for redfish with spinnerbaits—and buzzbaits— whenever the need for them arises throughout most of the year (like when I can't fly-fish for some reason and the use of a Dog is not feasible). For inshore purposes, they are possibly the most consistently effective redfish producers I have ever used—and that includes natural baits. And the "old faithful" gold spoons can't touch 'em in that setting! Take heed: to first catch a red, you must find him; then you must offer him something that will inspire him to eat. Spinnerbaits do that in spades!

CHAPTER 17

On Surface Lures

I have advocated the use of surface lures for reds throughout much of this book. Again, I must declare that they have played an important role in my successes with these fish, and I am therefore quite partial to them. So now I believe it's time for an in-depth review of them and their particulars. Believe me, reader, there is nothing in the world of fishing for reds that compares to targeting them with topwaters! And if you have ever heard, read, or seen anything that suggests that reds have "inferior" mouths and therefore don't dine on the water's surface very effectively, you have my explicit permission to suggest to the perpetrator of such garbage that he might benefit by removing his head from his butt!

I've read the Friday fishing report in the local newspaper for many years. It's reasonably helpful—each site listed in it references its particular hotspots and the best lures for enticing whatever has been biting during the past week, but it has become a bit predictable. In fact, it seems I have unintentionally memorized several of those reports almost verbatim!

You've probably read similar stuff: "Specks are doing well along the grass beds in Little Lake and over the oysters in Bay Round; reds are fair in the ponds off Big Creek, flounders are in the ditches and biting on the falling tide. Use live minnows for the specks and flounders; the reds want gold spoons"—the same as it was last week, the same as it was this time last year and will probably be again this time next year. So I was really floored when one Friday afternoon not long ago I read that topwaters were the lures of choice at several sites.

Actually it did my old heart good, as I have advocated their use for both specks and reds verbally and in magazine articles for many years. Still, I would not be so vain as to assume that those communications may have had anything to do with the lures' increasing popularity, though if they did, then that's great. In any case, the main thing is that more folks are using them to catch a lot of fish and have a lot more fun than they would have had while practicing other techniques.

If you recall, I do have a vested interest of sorts in topwaters, especially when they are being used for redfish. Besides having caught my first one on such a lure, literally hundreds of others have fallen to them—and a few hundred more to fly-rod poppers, which are also "topwaters," aren't they? Whatever, if you've caught them in this way before, what follows should still be interesting reading. If you haven't, then you've been missing out on one of the most productive ways of catching redfish there is, besides missing some of the most fun you can have with your white shrimp boots on! So if you are one of the latter types, I'd heartily recommend you consider what follows. And you may quote me here.

"Redfish will jump all over a surface lure just about any time they can detect one's presence." Believe it! Well, they will where I've been fishing, anyway.

That statement should tell you several things about where

and when a surface lure should be used, along with a hint or two about which types are usually most effective in different settings. Let's look at some old standbys as well as some of the newer types, and see which might be best in the different conditions that are commonly found along the coast.

First of all, though, you must understand that those conditions are what govern the fish's ability to detect the presence of these lures. Highly turbid water, rough water, and deep water (unless the fish are feeding near the surface) are no places for topwaters. Optimum depth for catching reds on them seems to be between roughly 2 and 3 feet. Subsurface visibility should be at least 1 foot—clearer is much better, and the water's surface should be almost smooth to only slightly choppy. Any radical departure from those conditions, and surface lures rapidly lose their effectiveness because of the increasing difficulty the fish have in locating them.

The Zara Spook has been a very popular surface lure for reds in some areas. That is undoubtedly because it's been around the longest. It's a big lure, a characteristic which is quite appealing. When twitched across the surface at a moderate or moderately fast pace, it looks just like a discombobulated mullet. In other words, it mimics big, easy prey. In clear water with only a slight chop, it remains a good choice, and these days the Spook also comes with rattles, which version is called a Super Spook. But there are others—newer types—which are at least as effective and which better cover more of the bases.

One of those—the Spit'n Image—was introduced to me a few years back by my friend Billy Murray, of Billy and Bobby Murray fame. If I remember right, he was on his first trip to my part of the coast, and a friend and I showed him around and put him on some fish. It turned out he fell in love with the place, and for a while we couldn't keep him away with a stick! But that aside, to show some of his gratitude he left me a handful of Spit'n Images, the lure not being on the market at that time.

The Image is considerably different from the Spook. It is smaller, but it is heavily weighted and can be cast long distances with little effort. It is best worked (as illustrated by Billy, who used it religiously and with great success) with an unbroken series of rather fast twitches, a retrieve which makes it skip across the surface like a frantic pogy. It also has rattles, an attribute that helps fish locate it in less than clear water. As I might have expected, I have found this lure to be best in interior ponds, bayous, and broken marsh where the water is less than 3 feet deep.

Spit'n Images, like several other surface lures, come in "junior" sizes. In my humblest of opinions, for saltwater purposes the only use they might have is in the shallowest water, where the impact of a larger lure might spook a nearby fish. I do have a couple of Image Jr.'s in my box, and on one gray, gut-slick summer afternoon in a particular shallow, crystal-clear tidal cut, I did catch several very nice reds on one of them. But for all-round redfishing in the aforementioned areas, I'll stick with the standard size, thank you very much.

And if there is even a hope of some big specks being around, I'll go to the even larger Top Dog.

My onetime best buddy, Capt. Bubby Rodriguez, turned me onto this lure on a February run for specks near my old home. I was fly fishing at the time—with poppers—and was enjoying more than enough explosive entertainment to make for a very good day. Bubby, choosing to fish with a casting rod, did equally well with a Dog. In fact, watching those fish strike it was almost more entertaining than watching them strike my popper! So I hied myself to town a few days later and bought a couple of them. That turned out to be a very strategic move, since on our next trip a brisk breeze made effective fly fishing impossible. On the other hand, the big surface lures accounted for near limits and generated plenty of the rambunctious shenanigans that the genre is infamous for.

And on our next trip, my first fish was a 28-inch red. I've been hooked solidly on that lure ever since.

The Top Dog is indeed a big—and heavy—lure, and upon looking at one for the first time, an aspiring topwater angler could easily become intimidated by it. Have no fear, folks, I've taken and been a part of taking plenty of rats on these lures as well as "bulls" up to 30 pounds or thereabouts. Try one, and you will be amazed at just how large a prey even a small fish will attempt to eat!

The Dog—and the junior size, which after nearly a decade now I am still attempting to determine the usefulness of—can be easily cast into the next parish (a.k.a. "county"), has a single rattle that emits a sound that quickly becomes addictive, and should be "walked" like a Spook. In my experience, it is more effective in deeper and slightly more turbid water than a Spook or Image, though it still works just fine in shallower and clearer water. It's a good lure for prospecting as well as for tossing into a known school of feeding reds.

One of my longtime favorites is the Skipjack. It is the smallest and lightest of the surface lures mentioned so far, but the model with the weighted tail, which I favor, makes a lot of fish-attracting racket with its aft propeller and its rattles. It is a good lure for reds in really skinny water, but I don't use it much anymore, preferring the newer and slightly heavier models, which generate fewer "professional overruns" on my casting reels. However, the Skipjack should be just right when combined with a light spinning outfit. Retrieve it at a moderate pace with short, sharp twitches—a steady staccato slosh-and-rattle beat—and enjoy their music. A big Ker-sploosh! will tell you that you are playing it just right.

There are quite a few other surface lures that are time-proven for saltwater use. The Jointed ThunderStick is one, though it typically sees more use enticing big specks than in prospecting for reds. This lure is worked differently from most of the others: you "rip" it for a short distance, causing it to dive a foot or so and wiggle such that its rattles really make some racket. Then as you pause to reel in the slack line all that created, and the lure floats back to the surface, where the procedure is repeated—provided it doesn't get blasted while it is sitting there!

Another favorite is the Jumpin' Minnow. To me, it is nothing more than a slightly streamlined Super Spook, but it "walks" nicely and makes pretty music. So does the Yo-Zuri lookalike— which costs about twice as much. As I have mentioned, the Devil's Horse that was mounted on a plaque and graced a wall in my loft for so long was not intended for reds but accounted for my first one back in 1964, and in the lip of a mounted red that was once nearby it was a fly-rod popper.

That latter lure—all right, "fly"—is a bit unlike the others I have discussed, as it pops while the rest slosh and rattle. For sure, there are "popping" lures on the market that will take reds, and I personally have caught exactly one on that type of lure—and that's it! I simply don't like 'em, but I absolutely adore fly-rod poppers. Let's just say it's a personality quirk and let it go at that.

And I will say nothing about those tiny wiggling surface lures that dive an inch or so beneath the surface, and received way too much hoopla a while back, except that, in my most humble opinion, they serve no real purpose.

Preferred colors can be another personal thing, but with surface lures there are some rules you should follow for best results. In clear water on bright days, mullet coloration—black or dark green over off-white—has been proven to work well, while on dark days and in slightly turbid water the lure should have a darker bottom. Or you can forget about all that and use a green-over-yellow combination. Hereabouts, at least, that's a good one!

To be most effective, any surface lure should be attached to the line with some form of loop. I ignore that excellent rule when fishing with fly-rod poppers, having no confidence in my ability (and in my aging eyes and fingers) to tie such a knot while in a boat. Likewise with a Dog. But I do install a small stainless split ring to the lure's line eye. That is every bit as functional as a loop knot is, allowing the lure to swing back and forth easily with every twitch of the rod tip. Some surface lures come with split rings already attached in that position; others don't. You would be wise to see to it that all of yours do. I prefer Lee SR5s (size 5).

Also, some lures' hooks may be fastened directly to eyes secured in their bodies. It is advisable to remove these hooks, as they are destined to bend—especially by redfish—and will weaken considerably when straightened. Install split rings—same type and size—on the eyes and replace the original hooks. For Dogs, I prefer a size 2 VMC 7650PS. Then, if one bends, little time is required to replace it, *not* straighten it!

Here's another consideration. Surface lures are popular with a lot of wading anglers, and anyone who has practiced that exercise for any length of time has probably had to painfully extract one or more of the lure's hooks from a body part—as I did

Replacing treble hooks on surface lures with short-shank,
single hooks makes it easier to release redfish.

(again) this past spring. Replacing those treble hooks with short-shank, single hooks such as a Siwash or Mustad C68S SS—the front one with its point down and the rear one with its point up—could save a wading angler a lot of grief. They are also much easier to retrieve from a big red's gullet than a treble hook is, and that's definitely good for the well-being of any fish you intend to release.

While surface lures can be every bit as productive as sinking lures, and while they do seem to offer a better chance for big fish—in the proper settings!—many of their advocates use them simply because watching the fish strike them is such a boot in the butt.

And that brings up another rule for using topwaters for reds: never attempt to set the hook until you actually feel the fish's weight. Reds—and specks for that matter, which you will assuredly entice while working water that is near the deep end of the preferred range—either have an uncanny ability to avoid those treble hooks, or they get as much enjoyment out of playing with their food as they do eating it. Whatever, missed strikes do occur, and if you jerk the rod back after one of them, jerk, you might jerk the lure so far away from the fish that it loses contact. Control yourself, wait until you feel him, and then jerk. Got that?

While the continuous retrieve is considered a standard with most surface lures, sometimes the fish will let you know that something needs to be done a little differently. One clue is several quick swirls behind the lure but no liquid explosion around it. Granted, that seems to occur more often with specks than with reds, but occasionally it seems that reds are a bit reluctant to commit—not often, but sometimes. Once again, contrary to what you may have heard, read, or seen elsewhere, if a fish reacts like that, stop the retrieve, allow the lure to rest idly for three or four seconds, and then give it just the slightest twitch. That really trips their trigger—and more than likely yours, too! It sure does mine.

As previously mentioned, missed strikes on the surface—though not especially common with reds—are just a part of the drill. Frequently, though, they are a result of the conditions confronting you—like a cloudy day with a chop almost rough enough to preclude the use of surface lures. In this case, slowing the retrieve a bit will allow the fish to take a better aim. On the other hand, on bright, slick-calm days a slightly faster retrieve will often generate "hunger strikes" instead of reluctant swirls and swats. If it doesn't, the sooner you switch to a spinnerbait, the better!

Still, unless conditions are really adverse—or unless I'm fly fishing—you will seldom find me prospecting for inshore reds anymore with anything other than a surface lure—usually a Dog. And that includes during the depths of winter and in some pretty chilly weather. Of course, "chilly" is some areas would be downright frigid hereabouts! The point is, when reds are in suitable water—whatever time of the year it is, they will strike a surface lure.

Just heed this warning. Don't let yourself freeze up as you gape in utter amazement at that big hole in the water where your Dog just sat, stammering "D-d-d-did you s-s-see that . . .?" You gotta get the hook set!

CHAPTER 18

Fly Fishing

Throughout these pages, I have made occasional references to fly fishing for reds. That's because it is a technique that has been dear to my heart for decades. It is also a technique that, in its time and place, is unbeatable in the fun-and-games department, and it can occasionally surpass the productivity of conventional methods.

Oh yes, it can!

I recall a particular early spring morning in the surf of the late and great Little Gosier Island in the Chandeleurs when my fly rod and I tallied 13 lovely reds—three of them assuredly well into double digits—while my five jig-slinging buddies accounted for a total of 30 between them. I don't remember who was top rod among them, but whoever it was, he wasn't bragging about it—not to me, anyway!

If I may gloat—er, "reaffirm" my stand on the subject, my largest red—36 pounds—was taken on a fly. So were—at this writing—nearly a thousand others. Granted, my largest fly-caught inshore red—a fish I mentioned earlier in these pages and weighing not quite 15 pounds—wouldn't rate a second look these days in areas where reds twice that size are relatively common, but when I caught it way back then it blew some minds. Incidentally, I caught it—and shortly thereafter another red surpassing 14 pounds—on a $7\frac{1}{2}$-foot, 6-weight outfit that cost in the neighborhood of $70 and could probably be matched these days for around $100! But more on suitable gear later.

I am also compelled again to note that the spot that gave up that grand fish also yielded my largest local bass—likewise taken on a popper—and, for a time, my largest speck, though that fine fish fell to a spinnerbait. It was quite a spot!

And that seems an excellent way to emphasize the point that some places are made to order for fly fishing, and some most definitely are not! Those folks who employ guides in order to experience this opportunity need not overly concern themselves with that particular point. On the other hand, it is perhaps the most

Fly fishing is one of the most enjoyable
and effective ways to catch redfish.

important aspect of the technique for freelancers, especially those who are just beginning to practice the exercise.

And on that note, like the old buddy who loaded his "ultralight" spinning reel with 14-pound mono, if you choose to adorn your Clouser Minnow with a dead shrimp and soak it all on bottom, then knock your lights out! However, if you want to fly-fish for reds, you should first have a good understanding of where and when to do so.

And right up front I beseech you to carry along a casting rod on your initial trips, just in case those aspects are not favorable for fly fishing. We sure don't want this to result in any dry runs!

Okay, to begin with, the weather and water conditions play a much more important role in fly fishing for reds than in conventional methods. Bright days and decent water clarity that combine for good subsurface visibility are a big help, and a breeze less than 15 knots or thereabouts is desirable—the calmer, the better. In my experience, anyway! If on your first fly-fishing ventures, any one of these three parameters is missing, then pitch a jig—shrimp-sweetened or straight up, it matters not in the least!

Juveniles

Although there are some marked exceptions, which seem to be increasing by the year, most of the reds found inshore are juveniles, and juvenile reds are creatures of the shallows. Those are often clear and sheltered from wave-creating breezes by various submergent and emergent grasses, shorelines, and the like. Such habitat occurs in areas of marsh, as well as along the edges of bays, and is made to order for fly fishing.

Clear, sheltered water is important here because it leads to easy detection of fish that are offering very little or no indication of their presence above the surface. Sight-fishing for them is preferred in this setting, as it is more exciting and less taxing physically than extensive blind-casting sessions, so any weather or water characteristic that will facilitate the exercise is desirable.

On that note, reds consume a lot of crabs and critters that are most often found on or near bottom. Nevertheless, they have absolutely no aversion to chasing down and eating prey near or at the surface. Shallow water therefore allows them to feed in both manners efficiently enough and also aids the angler by allowing the use of only a few flies. Fact is, in marshy or bay-edge waters under suitable conditions, a popper is very hard to beat! And again feeling the need to gloat just a little in order to stress a point, a bit over half my fly-caught reds fell to poppers. So, once again, if you hear something from a philistine about a red's mouth being "inferior" for surface feeding, don't believe it!

Most often, if weather and water conditions are favorable, you can successfully fly-fish for inshore reds in any place where you would prospect with a spoon or a spinnerbait. There has been a lot said in these pages about just that, so I won't repeat it here. Just remember that fly fishing is neither magic nor a cure-all, so don't try it or expect it to be productive in areas you would not fish with those types of lures.

While poppers attract reds by sound as well as by sight, sinking flies attract by sight alone—perhaps also by a bit of "push" in the water that can be detected through the fish's lateral line. The point is, flies generally have less drawing power than conventional lures do. That isn't too important when sight-fishing, but while blind-casting a promising area, you should cover it more thoroughly than you would with, say, a baited popping rig or a spinnerbait. Don't be in a hurry while blind-casting!

The way either type of fly is retrieved is important, not especially the pace and rhythm of it but how it's actually done. After the cast is made, the rod's tip should be pointed directly at the fly and held low to the water's surface. The retrieve is then created with short intermittent line strips, with the line being cradled just beneath the rod's grip with the forefinger of your rod hand. Upon a strike, you should therefore have no slack in the line between the rod tip and the fly, and the hook can be securely set with a single firm strip-strike. *Do not* raise the rod tip in an effort to set the steel; do so only after the fish has been hooked! That's a lot different from what one may have done over years of freshwater fly fishing, but when dealing with the generally bigger fish here and the bigger, stouter hooks that hold them best, it's a necessary task. Learn to do it!

Continuing along this line, if you have a reasonably sensitive forefinger on your rod hand, you can bring in a red just as you would a bass, by stripping in line when you can and using the finger for a "drag" if the fish makes a run. However, if you hook a wild one—or a big one—that takes off like the proverbial striped ape for somewhere way over yonder, you will need to get all slack line cleared and the fish on the reel, where it can be fought in a conventional manner. Practice this, even if the fish doesn't demand it.

Now to flies. Specialized patterns may be hot in particular areas along the coast, and it's wise to include a few of them in your stash. But there are a few others that should be in the fly box of everyone who fishes for reds wherever they are found inshore. The first is a popper—or rather, poppers. I'd recommend a few in sizes 4 or 2, between 2 and $2\frac{1}{2}$ inches long, and some in Nos. 1 and 1/0 between 3 and $3\frac{1}{2}$ inches long, the smaller ones being used for sight-fishing and the larger for blind-casting. Productive colors can vary widely with the location, but I'd be sure to have some of the smaller sizes in green over yellow and some of the big ones in chartreuse over white. Or you can match the color of the locally hot Dog!

Clouser Minnows, also in size 1 and about 3 inches long, are excellent blind-casting choices across the redfish's entire range. Chartreuse over white is probably the most productive color combination, but a few in solid purple may save a trip. That color is not commonly found in fly shops and mail-order catalogues, so you may have to coerce a fly-fishing buddy to tie some for you—only slightly weighted. They are worth the effort, especially on sunny but chilly winter days!

So there are four general patterns that work. You can load the box with others if you are so inclined, but while you are fishing with one of the four and not catching anything, you should change spots, not flies! Have I suggested that before?

As far as gear goes for inshore reds, an 8- or 9-weight outfit will allow you the best flexibility and even be adequate in the surf where the bulls roam. Fact is, the first known bull red to be caught on a fly in Louisiana waters was taken on a 9-weight, and fairly handily, too. Yeah, I caught it—and I'm damn proud of it! But that aside, if you intend to do most of your fishing in interior areas, spend the money on the best rod you can afford, and cut overall costs on the reel. A rod with a moderately fast action is a better choice here than a fast-action boom-stick. And one of those forged and gold-anodized things of beauty with a silky drag is awfully nice to fish with, but it certainly isn't needed here. Consider the outfits offered by such outlets as Cabela's and Bass Pro Shops—a decent one will cost about as much as a Calcutta reel and an All Star rod. A simple floating, weight-forward tapered line and 20-pound Dacron backing to fill the reel are sufficient.

Bulls

While interest in fly fishing for reds is growing rapidly in many areas, it seems to be centered mainly around juvenile fish in interior areas. That's a bit strange to me, because bull reds provide one of the best big-fish opportunities for fly anglers throughout the fish's range, and they are comparatively neglected.

That is certainly not because they are scarce or difficult to access. It appears to be in part because most folks associate fishing for them with adverse weather, with bait, or in or near deep, current-swept coastal passes. And it's most assuredly because these fish get big, and a lot of folks just can't comprehend catching big fish with fly tackle! For those and any others who have some aversion to fly fishing for bull reds, let me offer an attitude adjustment. Bull reds can be almost easy on fly—well, hooking them can be. After that, all hell usually breaks loose!

The key to it all is to find something in the water they inhabit that concentrates them, since prospecting for single fish seems to usually be a lesson in futility. There are two forms of structure that are found in proper habitat for fly fishing for bull reds—the surf—that serve that purpose very well. The first is a jetty extending seaward either for some distance or into water at least 15 feet deep, give or take a bit. The second is the pattern of troughs, bars, and pockets found in the surf zone itself.

If I simply had to go out and catch a bull red on a fly, my steps—or my boat's wheel-wash—would point toward a jetty. Any pile of large, usually granite boulders stuck out into the ocean quickly becomes a microcosm of sea life made up of resident prey and predators, as well as transients of both persuasions. As far as bull reds go, there are typically a few homeboys around such a structure that are joined—usually during late summer and autumn—by packs of temporary visitors. Or so has been my experience with them. In any case, all of them compete for the available food, and the more of them that are present, the more competitive they become—and the more likely it becomes that you will get your fly in one's face!

I prefer fly fishing a jetty from a boat while under trolling-motor power, and if that's neither safe nor sufficient in the prevailing sea conditions, I go somewhere else. Here, the best technique is to cast at a shallow angle to the rocks, placing the fly some 5 to 10 feet from them and allowing it to sink to increasing depths until you either hook a fish or a rock, counting the fly down all the while. In the first case, that's as far as you need to count on subsequent casts; in the latter case, don't count so far next time. And don't forget to set the hook with a line-strip, not by raising the rod!

.Just about any bull red encountered along a jetty can be handily tamed with a 10-weight outfit, but I prefer a 12-weight, mainly because I toss flies with it that I can't cast with the lighter stick. Those again are usually Clouser Minnows or similarities—weighted—tied on *sharp* size 4/0 hooks and between 5 and 5½ inches long. Olive over white and chartreuse over white are good choices. If you can throw one of those monstrosities 50 to 60 feet with a 10-weight, then that should be your choice.

While buying the best rod you can afford is again recommended here, it's also a good idea to buy a better reel than you did for inshore work. It should have a quality drag and capacity for an intermediate sinking line and at least 200 yards of 30-pound Dacron backing, and more is much better. You probably won't need all that for bull reds, but creatures other than them are often present around jetties, and if you happen to hook one—say, a 30-pound king mackerel—then you will definitely need it!

The troughs and bars found in the mainland surf and around barrier islands also serve as concentrating elements that aid in getting your fly in front of a fish, and you can fish them with flies just as you would with a casting rod and a spoon. Here, I now prefer a 10-weight outfit, though as I mentioned earlier, a 9-weight once sufficed nicely. My present outfit is comprised of a boom-stick, since reaching out and touching someone is often required, and the line is a floating type with a clear intermediate sinking tip. And the reel is top-of-the-line and holds a *lot* of backing—you can chase a bull on foot if it decides to run along the beach, but I draw the line a little past the second bar if the fish heads for the horizon! I've seldom had a surfside bull run more than 100 yards, but that extra backing makes retrieving the rest as the fish returns a lot easier. And on that note, if you can afford a decent large-arbor reel, buy it. It will allow you to retrieve line faster than you can with a standard-arbor reel.

Productive flies are again governed somewhat by the local preferences, but you cannot go wrong with a size 2/0, chartreuse-over-white Clouser Minnow. Sound like a broken record? Oops, I forget that many of you probably don't know what a "record" is. Whatever, the Clouser is tried and true in the surf—believe it!

One thing about fly fishing in the surf that isn't a problem when you are afloat: that rod is going to become very long and very awkward once the fish is close at hand. It's always best to beach a bull red, and while doing so, refrain from putting a deep bow in the rod, which can lead to its sudden catastrophic failure. You surely don't want that right at the time you are about to lay claim to a real fly-fishing trophy!

Reds—both the juveniles and the adults—are wonderful fly-fishing entertainment. They are available across a comparatively large area, and there are plenty of them, thanks at least in part to some pretty radical conservation measures. Apply the tips herein to the data in the earlier chapters on specific areas, and you will be well on the way to enjoying these fish to the absolute max.

Get after it!

CHAPTER 19

In Case You'd Like to Eat 'Em

The culinary value of redfish, at least in my opinion, decreases exponentially with their increasing size. The best tasting—and in many areas the most illegal to possess—are about a foot long; the worst tasting—and possibly the second-most-illegal to possess—are those exceeding around 10 pounds. Those that fall somewhere in between are best suited for the skillet—and the pot—and the grill! So, since there is absolutely nothing illegal, immoral, or fattening about eating a proper-sized redfish every now and then, I offer you some thoughts on preparing them for such an end.

Depending on your appetite, the smaller ones—say, 20 to 22 inches long—are best suited for the grill. The following entree, when served with potato salad, sliced tomatoes or asparagus spears, and a glass of chilled Vouvray, should suffice nicely for you and your wife/girlfriend/whatever.

Carefully fillet one such fish, but neither scale nor skin the fillets. Set those on a sheet of aluminum foil, scales down, make four evenly spaced, longitudinal slices across the fillet, ensuring they do *not* cut through the skin, and dust them moderately with garlic salt and lightly with red pepper.

In a small saucepan, slowly melt half a stick of margarine. Add to that one finely chopped, medium-size shallot, a table-spoon of lemon-pepper seasoning, and a half tablespoon each of fresh minced garlic and parsley. Stir it all together until it is well mixed, and let it sit on low heat for around 15 minutes, stirring it occasionally.

Now, either place the fillets—without the foil—scales down on a *hot* grill or on the foil (placed inside a cookie sheet if you so choose) in the oven that has been heated to around 500 degrees on broil. Baste the fillets right away, again around the time you figure you have ruined two perfectly good redfish fillets (after perhaps five minutes), and again at the time you can easily flake the meat. That means it's just about done and should take per-haps—hell, I don't know, until the meat flakes! You'll know. Serve the fillets scales down, and eat it by flicking the meat away from the skin. Yum!

Slightly larger fish—2 feet long or thereabouts—make pretty good skillet material. Carefully fillet the fish, skin the fillets, and then cut out any red meat that might be present. That done, cut the fillets into chunks about the size of a large fig—all right, a small lime. Something that will take a couple of bites to eat!

Place a cup or so of commercial fish-fry meal—or plain old yellow cornmeal—into a brown paper sack. Add a tablespoon (or a bit more) each of black pepper and salt, shake it all up real good, drop in the chunks, and shake it all up real good again.

Put enough peanut oil in a skillet to cover the chunks, add a

Smaller redfish, where legal, make the best eating. Always check local fishing regulations, and let the big bulls go!

few flicks of water, and heat it until the water begins to pop rather violently. The oil has to be hot! Then drop in the chunks—carefully!—and cook them until they are fork-tender and golden brown. Do not overcook them. Serve them with french fries, a couple of medium shallots on the side, and a very cold beer. If you like to dip your fish and fries in ketchup, first stir in a couple or three drops of Tabasco and Worcestershire— and a squiggle of lemon juice if you like. My wife and I used to have to eat like that when we were young and poor. Still do, too!

The fish on the big end of the scale are best when they are disguised a bit. A very good way to do that is to begin by preparing one as if you were going to fry it, but place the chunks in the foot of some pantyhose instead of the brown paper sack, being careful not to compact them too tightly. And yes, the pantyhose should have been previously washed! If you are still averse to that part of the recipe, you can buy "footlet"-type hose that work just as well. Tie a knot in the hose just above the chunks, and trim and discard the excess.

Put a gallon of water in a soup pot and season it with 2 table-spoons of Zatarain's Concentrated Liquid Crab Boil. Bring it to a boil, and drop in the hose-full of redfish chunks. Boil those for 35 minutes or so, drain them, and after they've quit dripping dump them into a large salad bowl. At that point I would discard the panty hose.

Bust up the chunks, then blend in a couple of good dollops of fat-free mayonnaise and three or four finely chopped shallots (that's green onions, in case you don't know). Stir it all up, let it cool in the fridge for an hour or so, and serve it on a bed of lettuce with tomato chunks around the edge and French bread on the side. Your choice of beverage, but the cold white wine (Vouvray) is pretty good with it. If you choose, you can garnish it all with a few shrimp you boiled with the fish chunks. Chop up some of them to blend into the salad, and save some whole for placing around the perimeter of the dish. It's unbelievably good either way, but I often feel the addition of the shrimp is sort of like putting ice cream on apple pie. Why mix two things that are perfectly good when they stand alone? Whatever, then there's Pete's bodacious redfish soup.

First, you make a roux. If you can't do that, then eat a salad.

Oh, all right, I'll teach you, but you have to have courage— and once you start, you can't stop to go pee, answer the phone or the door, or go to the fridge to fetch another beer. You must either go with it or toss it and start all over!

Again, begin by filleting, skinning, and cutting the redfish into bite-size chunks, then finely chop a large yellow onion and set a tablespoon of fresh minced garlic nearby. Now open a can of petite diced tomatoes and two cans of tomato sauce, and set them beside the dish your tablespoons of basil (smashed!), thyme, white pepper, onion salt, parsley, and two bay leaves are contained in. Now put a soup pot on the stove, add $\frac{1}{2}$ cup of corn oil and a few flicks of water to it, place a paper plate with $\frac{1}{2}$ cup of flour in it close at hand, and turn the heat under the pot up to high.

When the flicks of water start popping, immediately turn the heat down to medium and dump in the flour. Now you must stir it continuously (I prefer a wooden spoon for building a roux) until it turns a rich, dark brown and begins to smell like it's about to burn. At that point, quickly add the chopped onion. Continue to stir it constantly for three or four minutes and add the minced garlic. Keep stirring for another minute or so, and then dump in the tomatoes, the sauce, and four cups of water—still stirring. Don't stop! Now add all the spices but the parsley and stir them in for a minute or so, turn the heat down to low, cover the pot, and let it all simmer for about 30 minutes. Then add the chunks of fish and the parsley and simmer it all—again covered—for another half hour or until the chunks flake easily. Serve it as a soup over rice or pasta with toasted buttered French bread. It will make you slap your grandmomma!

I must declare that catch-and-release is a very worthwhile prac-tice—when practiced properly!—and I've turned loose a lot of redfish over the years, many of them being prime eating size. But after you try these four recipes, I'll just about guarantee you'll be practicing a little "catch-and-keep" in the future—occasionally, anyway.

Just do so within the limits of the law, if you please—and for Pete's sake, let the big bulls go. Compared to the others, they are not fit to eat!

Epilogue

So there it is. Undoubtedly I've omitted a few ways and means—things like how to catch bull reds on top of the Chesapeake Bay Bridge Tunnel during the third week in May and how to stay alive while fishing the mouth of Ocracoke Inlet in a November nor'easter on a hard-falling tide. Still, there should have been more than enough for you to understand how these wonderful fish work and how to catch them—and then, if you so choose, how to cook them. They really do make pretty good groceries—the smaller ones, mind you!

I don't enjoy them as I once did—neither catching them nor eating them. That's because, thanks to Katrina, I don't fish for them very often anymore, having been displaced from my beloved lower Mississippi River Delta which, for all practical purposes, no longer exists. But then, subsidence and coastal erosion were eating up the Delta long before that accursed storm was ever conceived. That's a real shame, but it's a part of "the way it goes," and if you choose to live by the ocean, well . . .

At this writing, it's been almost a year since I caught my last red, and you can be assured that I really do miss them—catching them, mostly. Still, I'm not all that far from 'em, and I feel fairly

Redfish country—the way it was, and the Good Lord willing, the way it will be.

certain that once I've become a little better acclimated to my new surroundings, I'll find 'em. That canoe of mine was rescued with barely a scratch on it! Strange how that worked. Anyway, paddlecraft, redfish, and I go back a long, long way, and I sincerely hope that there's still some of it lying ahead of us—all three of us.

That would be nice.

Index